An Introduction to Communication in the Classroom

The Role of Communication in Teaching and Training

James C. McCroskey

West Virginia University

Virginia P. Richmond

West Virginia University

Linda L. McCroskey

California State University, Long Beach

PEARSON

*Boston   New York   San Francisco   Mexico City
Montreal   Toronto   London   Madrid   Munich   Paris
Hong Kong   Singapore   Tokyo   Cape Town   Sydney*

Executive Editor: *Karon Bowers*
Series Editor: *Brian Wheel*
Series Editorial Assistant: *Jennifer Trebby*
Senior Marketing Manager: *Mandee Eckersly*
Composition and Prepress Buyer: *Linda Cox*
Manufacturing Buyer: *JoAnne Sweeney*
Cover Coordinator: *Kristina Mose-Libon*
Editorial-Production Coordinator: *Mary Beth Finch*
Editorial-Production Service: *Stratford Publishing Services, Inc.*
Electronic Composition: *Stratford Publishing Services, Inc.*

For related titles and support materials, visit our online catalog at www.ablongman.com

Between the time Website information is gathered and then published, it is not unusual for some sites to have closed. Also, the transcription of URLs can result in typographical errors. The publisher would appreciate notification where these errors occur so that they may be corrected in subsequent editions.

Library of Congress Cataloging-in-Publication Information

McCroskey, James C.
    An introduction to communication in the classroom : the role of communication in teaching and training / James C. McCroskey, Virginia P. Richmond, Linda L. McCroskey.
        p. cm.
    ISBN 0-205-39615-1
    1. Communication in education.   I. Richmond, Virginia P., 1949–
II. McCroskey, Linda L.   III. Title.

LB1033.5.M32 2006
371.102'2—dc22   2005046534

Printed in the United States of America.

10   9   8   7   6   5   4   3   2   1   10   09   08   07   06   05

Contents

Preface

In 1976, the senior author collaborated with H. Thomas Hurt and Michael J. Scott to write what became one of the first books (published in 1978) related to communication in the classroom. Much has changed in the last three decades. What has not changed is the profound need for professional educators to become familiar with the research and theory related to communication in the classroom that have been generated by scholars in the field of communication.

Teachers from prekindergarten through college and trainers in business, government, and adult education centers are professional communicators. Unfortunately, the majority of teachers and trainers have no formal education in the field of communication. Of those who have had some coursework in the field, the course they are most likely to have taken is public speaking. While such courses can be useful, they typically do not even introduce the student to the process of human communication as it exists in typical classrooms. As any experienced educator knows, most teachers and trainers do very little public speaking as such, but they are involved in communication virtually all day, every day. There is no teaching or training without communication.

This book was not designed to teach the prospective or in-service teacher or trainer "everything you always wanted to know about communication." As indicated in the title of the book, it is "An Introduction" to study in this field. It is intended to provide basic information with application to all teachers and trainers and to prepare the reader to profit from reading other writings in this field.

Since this book is seen as a first book in the field of communication for many readers, we have attempted to keep the reading level low. We have not presumed the reader knows anything about communication, or about instruction, or about the role of communication in instruction. We have attempted to explain most concepts so that the person who has never come into contact with the given concept before can still understand it. If you have some background, we hope you will just move quickly through explanations of things you already understand, while recognizing that what you already know may be a very new idea to other readers. When you have finished reading this book, we encourage you to read a more advanced book concerning communication in instruction: *The Handbook of Instructional Communication: Rhetorical and Relational Perspectives,* by T. P. Mottet, V. P. Richmond, and J. C. McCroskey (Boston: Allyn & Bacon, 2006). This book will take you into the research on instructional communication and the theories that research has generated.

Since we have team-taught courses dealing with communication in instruction with literally dozens of other faculty members and advanced doctoral students over the past 32 years, we are deeply indebted to many, many people for their ideas that are included in this book. Unfortunately, in many cases, we cannot even remember where some ideas originated, so crediting the origin of everything is not possible. Suffice to say, we are indebted to many present and former colleagues, as well as several thousand individuals who doubled as graduate students in our classes and teachers or trainers in their own. We would also like to thank Sherry J. Holmen of Albuquerque TVI Community College and C. M. Achilles of Eastern Michigan University, who reviewed earlier drafts of this material. This book represents our attempt to pass along what we have learned from all of these people to others who may be able to use such information to improve the learning of their students.

James C. McCroskey, West Virginia University
Virginia P. Richmond, West Virginia University
Linda L. McCroskey, California State University, Long Beach

About the Authors

James C. McCroskey received his B.S. Ed. from Southern State Teachers College in South Dakota. He majored in secondary education and received secondary teaching certification in English, Speech, and Mathematics. He received his M.A. degree from the University of South Dakota with a major in Speech Communication and a minor in Elementary Education. He received his doctorate from Pennsylvania State University with concentrations in Speech Communication and Educational Psychology.

McCroskey taught junior and senior high school English and Speech and coached academic debate teams in South Dakota for three years. For the past 45 years he has taught at the university level. He has taught at the University of Hawaii, Old Dominion University, Pennsylvania State University, Michigan State University, and Illinois State University. From 1972 to 1997 he served as the Chairperson of the Communication Studies Department at West Virginia University. Since that time, he has served as a Professor of Communication Studies and Educational Psychology at WVU.

He has received numerous awards for excellence in teaching, research, and service in the field of Communication Studies. He has received the Outstanding Teacher Award from West Virginia University and the Mentor Award from the National Communication Association, and he is a teaching Fellow of the Eastern Communication Association. He is one of the seven original Fellows of the International Communication Association and one of the five original research Fellows of the Eastern Communication Association. He is a past president of the Eastern Communication Association and a former Vice President of the World Communication Association. He has authored more than 50 books and more than 200 scholarly journal articles on communication in instruction, nonverbal communication, rhetorical communication, interpersonal communication, intercultural communication, organizational communication, persuasion, and argumentation. He has served as editor of four of the leading scholarly journals in the field of Communication Studies— *Human Communication Research, Communication Education, Communication Research Reports,* and the *Journal of Intercultural Communication Research.* He has received distinguished service awards from both the Eastern Communication Association and the World Communication Association. He has been honored as a Distinguished Research Scholar by West Virginia University and has received numerous research awards from professional associations in the fields of communication, teacher education, and pharmacy education. He has been recognized as the most prolific author of articles in leading research journals in communication studies in the nearly 100 years since the field launched its first journal.

Virginia P. Richmond received her B.S. from West Virginia Institute of Technology with majors in English and Secondary Education. She received her M.A. in Communication Studies from West Virginia University. She received her Ph.D. from the University of Nebraska with concentrations in Speech Communication and Management.

Richmond taught English in high school for two years. For the past 30 years, she has taught at the university level—at the University of Nebraska and Wheeling Community College, prior to joining the faculty at West Virginia University in 1977. Since that time she has served as a Professor of Communication Studies and Educational Psychology. Since 1979, she has served as Coordinator of Off-Campus Graduate Programs for the Communication Studies Department, and for three years she served as Coordinator of Extended Learning for the University.

She has received numerous awards for excellence in teaching, research, and service to the field of Communication Studies. She has received the Outstanding Teacher Award from West Virginia University, has been recognized as an outstanding teacher by both the Eastern Communication Association and the Western States Communication Association, and is a teaching Fellow of the Eastern Communication Association. She is also one of the five original research Fellows of the Eastern Communication Association. She is a past president of the Eastern Communication Association. She has authored 25 books and more than 80 book chapters and journal articles on communication in instruction, nonverbal communication, interpersonal communication, organizational communication, and health communication. She has served as editor of two leading scholarly journals in the field of Communication Studies—*Communication Quarterly* and *Communication Research Reports* (where she was founding editor). She has received a Distinguished Service Award from the Eastern Communication Association and has received numerous research awards from professional associations in the fields of Communication Studies, teacher education, and pharmacy education. She has been recognized as the fourth most prolific author of articles in leading research journals in communication studies in the nearly 100 years since the field launched its first journal.

Linda L. McCroskey received her B.A. from West Virginia University with a major in Communication Studies. She received her M.A. from West Virginia University in Communication Studies with concentrations in instructional and interpersonal communication and another M.A. from Arizona State University in Communication with concentrations in intercultural and organizational communication. She received her Ph.D. from the University of Oklahoma in Communication with concentrations in intercultural communication and organizational communication.

McCroskey is an Assistant Professor of Communication Studies at California State University in Long Beach, CA. Prior to taking the position at CSULB, she taught at West Virginia University, Arizona State University, Charlotte Community

College, James Madison University, and California Polytechnic State University. She also started and operated her own business for five years.

She has published articles in leading journals in the field of Communication Studies that focus on intercultural communication, instructional communication, and organizational communication. She serves as a reviewer for *Communication Quarterly,* the *Journal of Intercultural Communication Research,* and *Communication Research Reports.*

1

The Nature of Communication

Communication is central to the teaching/learning process. Knowledge is valuable in itself, but no matter how much one knows, there is no guarantee he or she can communicate that knowledge to others. Communication is the crucial link between a knowledgeable teacher and a willing student. From the vantage point of a professional educator, then, "the difference between knowing and teaching is communication in the classroom" (Hurt, Scott, & McCroskey, 1978).

While the centrality of communication in the teaching/learning process is obvious, that centrality is often ignored and frequently denied. In the late 1980s and early 1990s, a movement swept across the United States that ignored communication altogether. It focused on increasing the content knowledge of teachers. It manifested itself in new requirements for preservice teachers to have academic majors in the subject matter that they presumably would be teaching, even if their career objective was to teach first grade. An English, history, or mathematics major certainly will not hurt a prospective first-grade teacher, but it is not likely to be of much help, either.

The movement also manifested itself in "in-field" master's degree requirements for in-service teachers. The obvious and often stated objective of such requirements was to ensure that teachers would know enough to be able to teach the correct content to their students—certainly an appropriate goal. While it is true that there were, and most likely still are, some teachers passing on content that was out of date or simply wrong, it is also true that the overwhelming majority of teachers across the country are content-competent and in control of the subject matter.

After many years of teaching communication classes for in-service teachers, we have found that the most common problem reported by those teachers is not a lack of knowledge of the content they need to teach but, rather, that no one has taught them how to teach. It is a problem that is not recognized by many of these teachers until the first day of their teaching career. That is when they realize! As

1

Clair, a high school biology teacher with six years of teaching experience and tenure, put it: "I still have no idea how I should be teaching. I just do the best I can. Sometimes things seem to work, sometimes they don't."

Requiring Clair to go back to school for a higher degree in biology will not solve her problem. Helping her understand how to communicate with students, however, will go a long way toward providing a solution. The purpose of this chapter is to present a foundation for developing such an understanding. In the following sections we will be concerned with defining communication, identifying the key components of the communication process, and making some major distinctions that will be important for you to keep in mind while you learn about communication in the classroom.

Defining Communication

Over the past half-century, *communication* has become one of the most commonly used words in the English language. Like other words, it means different things to different people. We have computer communication. We study the communication of bees. We try to establish communication with people believed to live in other solar systems. We worry about what television communicates to our children. We are concerned that people from different cultures may have difficulty communicating with one another.

Communication is an integral part of the overwhelming majority of all jobs in the contemporary world. The telephone, telegraph, radio, television, book, magazine, and newspaper industries are communications fields. Communication is at the heart of the professions of law, the ministry, and, of course, teaching. All careers involving sales of any type of products or services are communication occupations.

Given these many different applications of the term *communication*, it might appear that people could have many different meanings in mind when they use the term. In fact, however, the term is used in only two very different ways.

Communication is sometimes used to refer to the process of transferring messages from one place to another. This is its use in the so-called communications industries noted earlier—telephone, television, publishing, and the like. The plural form—*communications*—is generally used in this context. Here, the term may also be used as a substitute for the more common term *messages*. For instance, if a technology component (your fax machine) picks up a message (or communication), transmits it over a wire or through the air, and delivers it to a receiver (another fax machine) in a form in which it can be reproduced, then communication has occurred. The focus in this case is on getting messages from one place to another.

This is not the kind of communication with which we are concerned here. When we are trying to teach students, we care about more than just moving messages. We are concerned, too, with *meanings* students have for those messages.

A concern for meaning is central to the way we will use the term *communication*. In this book, we will use the term to refer to *the process by which one person stimulates meaning in the mind of another through verbal and/or nonverbal messages.* Thus, teachers communicate with students by stimulating meaning in their minds, and students communicate with teachers by stimulating meaning in the teachers' minds. Of course, these communication processes can occur at virtually the same time.

To understand this definition of communication more fully, it is helpful to distinguish among three types of meaning-centered communication: accidental, expressive, and rhetorical.

Accidental Communication

This type of communication occurs when one person stimulates meaning in the mind of another without having any intention of doing so and, in many cases, without even knowing that he or she has done so. This type of communication occurs constantly in classrooms. Both teachers and students communicate their interest (or lack of interest), their backgrounds, their biases, and their weaknesses without having the slightest desire to do so—and often in spite of a definite desire *not* to do so. Most often, such accidental communication occurs as a result of nonverbal behaviors. The tone of a student's voice, a teacher's avoidance of the touch of a child with dirty hands, a student's late arrival at class, a teacher's smile when a student explains that "the dog ate my homework," a student's gaze out the window while the teacher is trying to get her or his attention, the teacher's wearing a beard, the student's coming to class in ragged clothing—all of these behaviors, and thousands more, are likely to result in accidental communication.

Expressive Communication

This type of communication arises from the emotions or feelings of the individual. Messages are generated that express the person's feelings. Sometimes this may happen as a result of a desire to communicate those feelings to someone else. This intent, however, is not an essential characteristic of expressive communication. A person can, for example, write a poem to express her or his feelings. The writer may have no desire to have other people read that poem, but if someone does, expressive communication is likely to occur. Similarly, circumstances may have a strong impact on our emotions, and we may spontaneously exhibit anger, fear, happiness, or a wide range of other emotions. If someone else is present, it is likely that the person will consider our behavior meaningful and perceive our emotional state. We may exert control over our expression of emotions so that people will think we have emotions that we do not really have. Acting as though we are surprised at the surprise party we have known about for a week is a good example. Teachers often learn to express emotions, particularly around small children, to meet the needs and expectations of others. When these are authentic emotions, they clearly represent expressive communication. When they are exhibited but not felt, they may move into the third category: rhetorical communication.

Rhetorical Communication

This is the type of communication with which we are primarily concerned in the classroom. With rhetorical communication, we are trying to get another person to form a specific meaning in her or his mind. Rhetorical communication is goal directed. It seeks to produce specific thoughts, feelings, and/or perceptions in the mind of another person. This is what teaching is about. As teachers, we want to get students to understand, believe, think, feel, and do. We try to influence them in terms of their perceptions, feelings, attitudes, and behaviors. In much the same manner, our students attempt to influence us. Thus, rhetorical communication is initiated by both teachers and students within the classroom. In large measure, the more effective the teacher is at rhetorical communication, the more effective he or she will be as a teacher.

The Instructional Communication Process

Figure 1.1 presents a model of the instructional communication process. This is one of the two principal forms of communication that regularly occur in the classroom; the other is interpersonal communication, to which we will direct attention later in this chapter. We will reference this model to identify the critical components of the instructional communication process and to identify factors related to instruction that, though not communication components themselves, nevertheless may have a major impact on the effectiveness of teachers' communication. Let us examine each component.

Source

The source is the person who originates a message. In instructional communication, the primary source is the teacher, although students also initiate messages. Before the teacher begins to communicate, however, there are critical concerns that must be addressed. These precommunication activities relate to setting the agenda for the instruction that will follow. They are (1) setting the major goal or goals for an instructional unit, (2) choosing the general objectives to be achieved, and, most important, (3) selecting the specific objectives that are to guide the instruction: cognitive (knowing, understanding), affective (feeling), and psychomotor (doing). A given instructional effort may not include all three types of objectives, but all must be considered. No matter how skilled a communicator the teacher may be, if he or she does not know what the student is expected to learn, the chance that the teacher will have any meaningful positive impact on the student's learning is dramatically reduced.

Encoding.   We suggested earlier that communication is the process by which a teacher stimulates meaning in the mind of a student through verbal and nonverbal messages. When the teacher has determined the meanings that need to be triggered,

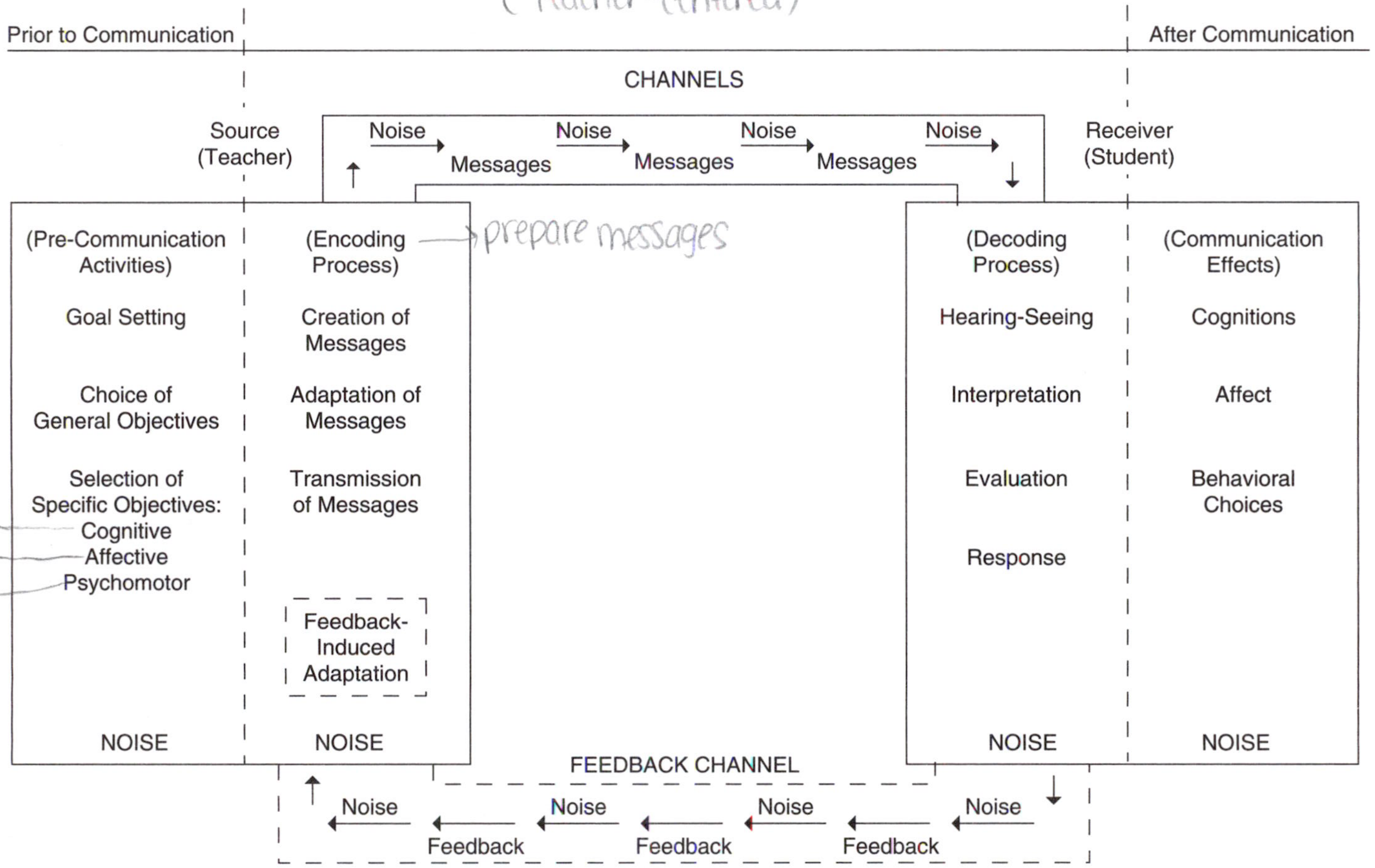
Prior to Communication
After Communication
CHANNELS
Source (Teacher)
Noise
Messages
Noise
Messages
Noise
Messages
Noise
Receiver (Student)
(Pre-Communication Activities)
Goal Setting
Choice of General Objectives
Selection of Specific Objectives:
Cognitive
Affective
Psychomotor
NOISE
(Encoding Process)
Creation of Messages
Adaptation of Messages
Transmission of Messages
Feedback-Induced Adaptation
NOISE
(Decoding Process)
Hearing-Seeing
Interpretation
Evaluation
Response
NOISE
(Communication Effects)
Cognitions
Affect
Behavioral Choices
NOISE
FEEDBACK CHANNEL
Noise
Feedback
Noise
Feedback
Noise
Feedback
Noise

FIGURE 1.1 *Instructional Communication Model*

the time has come to begin the encoding process. *This is the process by which teachers prepare messages that they believe will lead to the achievement of their specific objectives.* The process includes (1) creating the messages, (2) adapting the messages to the students, and (3) transmitting the messages.

Central to this process is the need to adapt the messages to the students. If the teacher simply expresses ideas in messages that represent the meanings in her or his own mind, those messages may mean little or nothing to the student who hears them. Because meanings cannot simply be passed from one person to another, we must put our meanings into codes, represented by verbal and nonverbal messages, that will be understood by others, who will then have meanings in their minds that are similar to ours. This is a critical facet of the communication process itself. If, as teachers, we present our ideas in codes that are inappropriate for our students, they will not achieve the learning objectives we have set. Messages must be understandable to the students for us to communicate with them and achieve our instructional goals.

Messages.   *Messages are verbal and nonverbal behaviors that have the potential to stimulate meanings in people's minds.* Words and groups of words may form messages. This is the type of message creation that is of concern in much of elementary and secondary education. Instruction about the nature and use of language is a central factor in teaching the young in most cultures. Much less studied but at least as important are the various nonverbal behaviors to which people attribute meaning. Tone of voice, eye behavior, a smile, a touch, and our use of space are just a few of the enormous array of nonverbal behaviors involved in human communication. Nonverbal behaviors will be the central focus of a later chapter in this book, so we will not go into this area in detail here. Suffice it to say that teachers' nonverbal behaviors provide potent messages to which students attend, and that these behaviors have an important impact on the communication between teachers and students.

Channels.   *Channels are the means by which messages travel from sources to receivers.* The basic human senses can serve as channels. Sound waves and light waves permit others to hear and see our messages. Electronic and print media also function as channels for messages. You are receiving this message via a book. Other messages travel via television, radio, film, telephone, and so on. People, too, can serve as channels. If Tom tells Mary, and Mary tells Pat, Mary has served as a channel between Tom and Pat.

Let us summarize the components of instructional communication that we have considered so far. We have indicated that *sources* (teachers) determine what they wish to communicate and then *encode* what they believe are appropriate *messages*, which they then send through various *channels* to one or more *receivers* (students).

Receiver

Receivers are the persons for whom the source creates messages. In instructional communication, students are the primary receivers, although teachers also receive messages from students. If the message reaches the student, he or she will engage in the process of decoding.

Decoding.   The decoding process has four essential parts: hearing-seeing, interpretation, evaluation, and response.

1. *Hearing-seeing.* The first step in the decoding process is always either hearing or seeing the messages, or both. When a teacher talks to a class, each student not only hears the words the teacher says but also experiences the teacher's facial expressions, tone of voice, gestures, and so on. If the student does not pay attention to the teacher, the instructional communication process dies. Hence, maintaining the student's full and favorable attention is crucial if the teacher hopes to facilitate student learning.

2. *Interpretation.* Interpretation, the next step in the decoding process, refers to the actions of the student in determining what he or she believes the teacher meant by the messages that were received. This assumes the student usually makes a conscious attempt to interpret the messages correctly. This does not mean, of course, that an interpretation that the teacher would consider correct is always the result. The student, however, will think this interpretation is right and may respond by using it as an answer on a test later on. When a student gives an answer that the teacher cannot imagine any student giving, it is usually the result of a misinterpretation during the decoding of the teacher's messages.

3. *Evaluation.* Once the student has interpreted what the teacher meant by the messages received, the messages are evaluated in terms of their meaning for the student. Tom may interpret the messages as the teacher asking him to do extra studying that evening. He might then consider whether such a behavior would be in his best interest or whether, for example, he might find watching television more desirable. Similarly, Heather may understand that the teacher said that Columbus had three ships in his expedition. However, she may decide that such information is mere trivia. Her negative evaluation will probably mean that she will not be able to recall that information later.

4. *Response.* Once the evaluation is complete, the student responds to the messages as they have been received, interpreted, and evaluated. This response may be observable by the teacher, or it may be covert. Sometimes both types of responses can occur, and they may not be in agreement with each other. For example, the student may respond by telling the teacher he or she will study that night, while actually having no intention of doing so.

Once the receiver has responded, the decoding process is complete, as the overall instructional communication process may be. Whatever impact the process will have on student cognitions, affect, and/or behaviors has been set in motion. Examination of our model of the instructional communication process, however, indicates there are important elements that we have not yet discussed: feedback and noise.

Feedback.   *Feedback is a student's overt response to a teacher's message.* In our model we see a feedback channel that includes arrows indicating that messages run through this channel from the receiver back to the source. The feedback channel is outlined in broken lines, in contrast to the primary channel, which is formed with solid lines. This is done to indicate that the primary channel must be present for instructional communication to occur. The feedback channel, however, may or may not exist, depending on such factors as the number of students being taught simultaneously or the presence of a medium (like television) through which messages must be transmitted.

Feedback is very important because it can have a significant impact on the effectiveness of the total communication process. We will consider feedback in more detail in a later chapter, so we will not cover it at length here. It should be noted, however, that student feedback is the primary source of information for helping teachers determine their ongoing effectiveness. Feedback indicating that students do not understand should be dealt with promptly so as not to discourage them from giving their attention to future messages.

Noise

The final component in our model of the instructional communication process is noise. It appears all over the place in the model—in the source, in the receiver, and in the channels. It appears before the process begins and continues even after it has ended. Noise is not, however, an essential part of the instructional communication process. In fact, we must do our best to reduce its presence. *Noise is any element that interferes with the generation of the intended meaning in the mind of the receiver.* Unfortunately, noise is almost always present.

Two types of noise can occur within the teacher. The first is what we might call "foggy thinking" about what meaning needs to be communicated. When teachers do not carefully prepare by determining the objectives the students need to meet, there is nothing relevant to guide the teacher's encoding. A unit of study may be presented to students simply because the teacher happens to like the content. This often leads to messages that are not adapted to students, and thus to very little student learning—however much the teacher may enjoy presenting the messages. Feedback may take the form of "Why are we studying this?" or "Is this going to be on the test?" Or it may take the form of lack of attention. Few teachers enjoy such feedback! Another example of this type of noise occurs when the teacher really doesn't understand the content that is to be taught. He or she may think it is clear, but it may be distorted and only partially understood. At best, under such circumstances, students will only partially understand the messages that the teacher is sending.

The second type of noise within the teacher is in the encoding process. This type of noise can occur when the teacher does not understand the encoding process itself, does not comprehend the psychology of the students, or does not have a grasp of where the students stand with respect to the content, in terms of both cognition and affect. Under any of these circumstances, it is likely that messages will be developed that are not appropriately adapted to the students.

Noise in the channel is often "noise" in a more literal sense. If an electronic medium is being employed, there may be "static" or "snow" that clouds the messages being sent. In a normal classroom, sounds, sights, and smells that are unrelated to what is being taught often demand the attention of students or make the processing of messages difficult. The classroom itself may introduce noise into the process through such things as inappropriate temperature, uncomfortable (or too comfortable) seating, and distracting bulletin board displays. Other students in the classroom also have a high probability of introducing noise for any given individual.

Noise in the receiver is at least as likely to disturb communication as noise in the source. Noise in the students is generated by their attitudes, beliefs, values, previous learning experiences, desires, motives, needs, and so on. When light switches are turned on, they invariably produce light (unless the electricity is off or the bulb is burned out). Similarly, when messages are received, they invariably produce responses, but these responses are far from perfectly predictable. The psychology of the receiver is a very noisy factor in the instructional communication process.

The Interpersonal Communication Process

Figure 1.2 presents a model of the interpersonal communication process. A very large portion of the communication that occurs in many classrooms is interpersonal. In this type of communication, the roles of source and receiver are constantly changing. Teacher and student each perform both source and receiver functions. Much of this kind of communication is not directed specifically toward teaching or toward learning specific objectives. That is not to say that it is unimportant, however. Some of it is directly related to formal instruction; the rest provides the context in which all learning takes place.

It is important to recognize that although the instructional communication model we have examined recognizes feedback and teacher–student interaction, it is primarily a teacher-dominated, one-way communication model. It presumes that the teacher has ample time for instructional planning and that lessons can be carefully developed and adapted for communication with the intended students. This model fits the typical college or university lecture course, in which it is common for a teacher to have more than a hundred students and not unusual to have two to four hundred, with a teacher occasionally having as many as a thousand students, if a large enough lecture hall exists. In such classes, it is not assumed that the teacher will know the individual students, let alone have any ongoing interaction with anyone in the class. Feedback-induced adaptation, then, is based primarily on testing and other forms of formal feedback rather than on responses of individual students.

By contrast, classes with small enrollments often involve a lot of interpersonal communication. Particularly in schools with intact classrooms, where one teacher instructs the same students all day, and in schools where the teachers work with the same students for a period of time each day or several days a week, students and teachers develop an ongoing relationship. As such a relationship develops, more

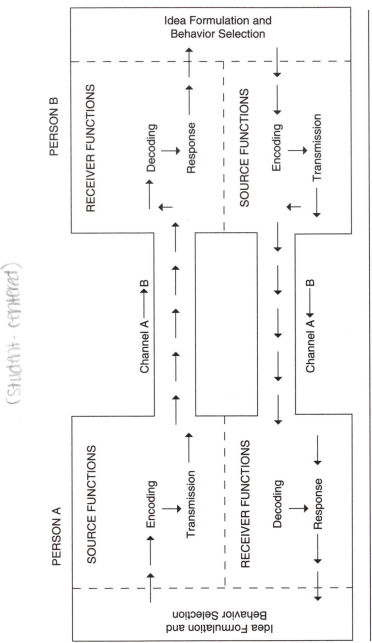

Relational Model
(Student-centered)

FIGURE 1.2 *Interpersonal Communication Model*

10

and more of what each person says or does is interpreted by the other in the context of the relationship. The relationship, then, becomes part of the instructional communication process and must be taken into account by the teacher who hopes to be effective. Interpersonal feedback, then, provides the information the teacher needs to adapt to the individual needs of the student.

Some Important Distinctions

Now that we have identified the major components of the instructional communication process and have related instructional communication to other communication that may occur in a classroom, it is important to emphasize a few distinctions that were made in passing.

Intentional Versus Accidental Communication

We have noted that instructional communication is a process involving intentional, volitional actions done by professional educators. This means that the teacher selects the goals and objectives that he or she intends to assist the student in meeting and carefully plans her or his communication with the student to ensure that the desired outcomes occur.

Of course, there are some teachers who fail to engage in such planning and careful monitoring of their communication behavior but still have students who accomplish the desired learning objectives. In such cases, the outcome is merely a case of serendipity—a fortunate accident. Regrettably, much of the learning that occurs in our schools is a function of just such fortunate accidents. Some students may learn not because of their teachers, but in spite of them. Other students who have the same teacher may learn little or nothing.

Our purpose in this book is not to stamp out serendipity. We are quite willing to accept the achievement of desired learning objectives even when they are produced by accident or through actions that seem ill advised. However, our goal is to help teachers foster student achievement by intentionally engaging in communication behaviors that, on the basis of research, appear likely to lead to such outcomes, while avoiding behaviors that may do so only by accident. Some accidents may produce desirable outcomes, but most do not.

> "One should never forget that learning by trial and error involves a lot of trials and a lot of errors, but only a little learning."

Expressive Communication Versus Rhetorical Communication

We have already noted the distinction between expressive and rhetorical communication, but it is important to emphasize it. Expressive communication is source-centered, whereas rhetorical communication is receiver-centered. Instructional communication is rhetorical by design. An exchange between two faculty members is illustrative:

> *First faculty member:*   How was your class this morning?
>
> *Second faculty member:*   It was good for me!
>
> *First faculty member:*   Huh?

Obviously, the second faculty member is trying to be funny. The attempt at humor catches the first faculty member off guard. We don't ask this kind of question expecting a teacher to tell how he or she feels; we expect to hear how the student responded or how the interaction in the class went.

It is not all that uncommon, however, for teachers to use their classrooms as a forum for expressing their attitudes or feelings, or for making elaborate explanations of small aspects of the lesson content that happen to fascinate the teacher but leave the students in a state of confusion. It may indeed be "good for" the teacher. But such communicative behaviors should not be confused with instruction.

Instructional communication is directed purposefully toward helping students attain desirable learning objectives. Other types of communication can and do exist in the classroom and may be very important to those involved in the communication. But if we are to measure the success of our schools by the amount our students learn, instructional communication should be the primary type that occurs in our classrooms.

Content Choices Versus Communication Choices

Whether they teach in kindergarten, in college, or at General Motors, professional educators must make many decisions that have an impact on their students. Some of these decisions deal with the learning objectives the students need to reach and hence what they need to be taught. Other decisions deal with how to help the students attain those learning objectives and hence how to communicate with the student. It is important that teachers be able to distinguish clearly between these types of choices and that they make each choice well.

The formal study of the role of communication in instruction is still a comparatively new area in the field. Therefore, it is sometimes misunderstood both by specialists in other areas of the communication field and by people whose academic experience has centered in another field, such as education. To put this new area of study into perspective, it is useful to look at content and communication choices and the kind of knowledge that informs each type.

Content Choices.   What students need to be taught in a given subject, say mathematics, should be determined by the expertise of people who specialize in the content field, in this case mathematics, and those who specialize in the fields of educational psychology and curriculum development. The former group may be most helpful in determining the general goals and objectives that students should be able to reach by the time they complete their work at a certain level (elementary school, high school, four years of college); the latter may be most helpful in determining the sequencing of such learning to meet the abilities and interests of students at various developmental and instructional levels. Clearly, specialists from the field of communication have little to offer in this area unless, of course, the subject matter to be taught is communication. Then their expertise is as critical as that of the specialists in mathematics in our previous example.

Communication Choices.   How to teach the content that has been chosen and how to communicate with the students so they will achieve the selected objectives should be informed by the expertise of people who specialize in pedagogy and those who specialize in communication (specifically, instructional communication). Experts in pedagogy are most helpful in designing appropriate systems of instruction that are geared to the type of content and academic level of the students. Specific pedagogical techniques and strategies have been developed and tested for many specific fields, as have general approaches. Experts in instructional communication are most helpful in identifying orientations, behaviors, and specific communicative approaches that teachers should employ (or avoid) to enhance student learning.

Clearly, the teacher needs to develop many types of expertise to optimize effectiveness. All are important, and the lack of any one may cause reduced effectiveness or even failure. Knowledge of content cannot be substituted for knowledge of pedagogy. Knowledge of pedagogy cannot be substituted for knowledge of communication. Knowledge of communication cannot be substituted for knowledge of subject-matter content. Hence, the focus of this book is on the communication choices that teachers must make. Although we may occasionally need to draw from other fields, such as educational psychology or pedagogy, we will do so primarily to show their relationships to our communication perspective on instruction.

References

Hurt, H. T., Scott, M. D., & McCroskey, J. C. (1978). *Communication in the classroom*. Reading, MA: Addison-Wesley.

McCroskey, J. C. (1968). *An introduction to rhetorical communication*. Englewood Cliffs, NJ: Prentice Hall.

McCroskey, J. C., Larson, C. E., & Knapp, M. L. (1971). *An introduction to interpersonal communication*. Englewood Cliffs, NJ: Prentice Hall.

Glossary

accidental communication   The stimulation of meaning in a receiver without the intention of doing so.

channels   The means by which messages travel from sources to receivers.

communication   The process by which one person (or group) stimulates meaning in the mind of another (or others) through verbal and/or nonverbal messages.

communications   The process by which messages from a source are transmitted to a receiver via electronic or print media over time and/or space. Also known as "mediated communications."

decoding   The process by which a person (or group) who receives a message interprets, evaluates, and responds to that message.

encoding   The process by which a person (or group) creates messages that may stimulate predetermined meanings in the mind of another (or others).

expressive communication   Verbal or nonverbal messages that arise from the emotions of an individual and that are decoded by a receiver.

feedback   A receiver's overt response to a source's message.

instructional communication   The process by which a teacher stimulates meaning in the mind of a student or students through verbal and/or nonverbal messages.

interpersonal communication   Interaction between two or more people in which each participant plays both the source role and the receiver role.

message   Verbal and/or nonverbal behaviors that have the potential to stimulate meanings in people's minds.

noise   Any element that interferes with the generation of the intended meaning in the mind of the receiver.

receiver   The person or persons for whom a source creates messages.

rhetorical communication   The intentional process of creating and transmitting verbal and/or nonverbal messages that are designed to stimulate predetermined meanings in the mind of another or others.

serendipity   A fortunate accident; a positive outcome that is not planned or foreseen.

source   The person (or group) that originates verbal and/or nonverbal messages.

2

Communication Conceptions and Misconceptions

As you were reading the first chapter of this book, you may have been puzzled by some of the comments made about messages and meaning. If you have never taken a social science–based course in communication, it is even more likely that you had difficulty with some of the ideas expressed. Do not be concerned. You are not alone.

Even if you had not taken a course or read a book in a given subject area, it is highly likely that you would have some idea of what the course or the book will be about. Think back to your first course in sociology, psychology, calculus, physics, or geography. You probably had some preconception of what a book for that course would include. However, it is most likely that as you got into the class, you discovered that some of your earlier conceptions were just plain wrong, or at least partially incorrect.

Approaching the study of communication, particularly instructional communication, is likely to produce this kind of phenomenon. Of course you know what communication is. You knew long before you read the previous chapter. You knew what it was even when you were a young child, right? Most people think they understand communication, because they are involved in it every day. Unfortunately, many of these understandings, or conceptions, are fuzzy at best and often so misleading as to make a person a very ineffective communicator. Before we go any further, please complete the short true–false Communication Background Test presented in Figure 2.1.

In our experience with large groups of elementary and secondary teachers, as well as with college students, professors, and administrators, we have found the responses to this test to be highly variable. Responses in all of the groups have varied from all items marked true to all items marked false, with the large majority marking from three to six items as true. Using our key for the correct answers, we found that the overwhelming majority of all of these groups received a D or an F on

---

COMMUNICATION BACKGROUND TEST

This is a brief test of the background knowledge you have about communication. Please respond by circling the "T" for true or the "F" for false before each statement to indicate whether your background and experience with communication indicates the statement is true or false. No maybes are permitted! There are only ten statements, so this test should only take you a few moments to complete.

1. T F   Words have meaning.
2. T F   Communication is a verbal process.
3. T F   Telling is communicating.
4. T F   Communication will solve all our problems.
5. T F   Communication is a good thing.
6. T F   The more communication, the better.
7. T F   Communication can break down.
8. T F   Communication is a natural ability.

FIGURE 2.1   *The Communication Background Test*

---

this test. Because "maybe" and "it depends" are not acceptable answers on this test, all eight of the statements are false. If you received a perfect score on this test, you have probably studied communication as a social science, or you heard about the test in advance! In either case, congratulations. You are not an ordinary person. You see, ordinary people (at least those without a background in the field of communication) are taught in this society that these statements are true.

Before we go too far, it is important to stress that the scores on this test are not really very meaningful. Whether you obtained a high score or a low score says little about your ability to communicate. The scores really only reflect how many culturally ingrained conceptions about communication you have been taught to believe. And we want to stress that although we believe "false" is a better answer than "true" for each of these statements, that does not mean there is not a glimmer of truth in any of them. Rather, we believe there are alternative conceptualizations that are far more useful for developing an understanding of instructional communication. The remainder of this chapter will be devoted to looking at the misconceptions represented on the test and alternative conceptions that may be more useful.

Misconception One: Words Have Meaning

The idea that meanings are in words is probably the most commonly held misconception about communication. The most serious problem with this notion in the context of instructional communication is that it can lead a teacher to believe that by giving students words, he or she has communicated to the students the meanings he or she has intended for the words. What a particular word means to you may not be what it means to someone else. The word stimulates a meaning in our minds that may be very different from the meaning it stimulates in the minds of our students. Depending on the context, the age, or the ethnic background of the user of the word, *hot* may mean "cold" or *cold* may mean "hot"; *bad* may mean "good" or *good* may mean "bad"; and so on.

Words also are frequently used in different ways in different academic fields. Compare our explanation of *feedback* in Chapter 1 with the way that term is used in physics. Or compare the way the term *science* is used by physical and biological scientists with the way it is used by social and behavioral scientists. Based on our discussion of the meanings of *communication* in Chapter 1, compare how people in the telecommunications industry use this word with the way it is used in this book.

Because of the way we are educated about words from early in life, we fail to realize and understand that words are merely codes or symbols for meanings we have in our mind. The meanings we have for words are the products of our culture, ethnic group, social class, and experiences. Thus, no two people share precisely the same meanings for all words, because no two people share exactly the same background and experiences.

Here's another way to look at things: *Meanings are in people, not in words.* This conceptualization of meanings locates them in the only place they can exist: in people's minds. Remember your exasperation in about the fourth grade when you went to your teacher and asked what some word meant? If your experience was like most people's, you were told, "Look it up in the dictionary." While it is important for children to learn how to use a dictionary, such injunctions by trusted teachers are likely to lead us to believe that meaning exists in words and that all we have to do to find it is to "look it up in the dictionary." Of course, when we do, we probably find the word is used in many different ways, so we still are at a loss as to what the word "means."

When we are preparing to communicate with our students, we need to concern ourselves with what a word or phrase might mean to them, not what it "means" in the dictionary. If we are not sure what the students might take the word to mean, we need to explain how we are using the word, what it means to us. This will help them share the "code" we are using to communicate a meaning to them. Whenever teachers and students do not share meanings for words, the use of those words is unlikely to help the student achieve the intended objectives.

Misconception Two: Communication Is a Verbal Process

When most people think of communication, they think of words, either written or spoken. This verbal focus is reasonable, given that our educational system stresses it from kindergarten through college. Most of education is devoted to words. So why on earth would we call this statement a misconception?

Communication is not just a verbal process. *Communication is a verbal and nonverbal process.* What we say is important, but often how we say it is of much greater importance. In addition, what we are doing before, during, and/or after we speak can be of even greater importance.

When we focus strictly on words, we may miss most of what is going on. Our vocal inflection tells others how to interpret our words. A statement with a wink should be taken differently than the same statement without the wink. An expression of condolence with a hug is far more powerful than the same expression without the hug. A description of a historical battle presented in a monotone is far less likely to be remembered by a student than the same description presented in a lively and animated manner.

To a large extent, our nonverbal behaviors are the determining factor in whether the words we use will stimulate the meanings we want them to stimulate. Verbal and nonverbal messages often serve different but highly complementary functions. We use words primarily to communicate cognitive or content meanings. We use nonverbal behaviors primarily to communicate affective or relational meanings. Although it is an overgeneralization, we may look at words as the "thinking" component of communication and nonverbal behaviors as the "feeling" component of communication. The feeling aspect provides the context for understanding the content. In the realm of instruction, it is critical that teachers communicate content with positive feelings, both for the content and for the student. If either is communicated negatively, it is likely to cause the student to reject the instructional transaction, with a resulting decrease in cognitive learning. Because nonverbal aspects of communication in the classroom are so important, we have included an entire chapter on nonverbal behavior in this book.

Misconception Three: Telling Is Communicating

Many people believe that simply saying or telling something is communicating it. As teachers, we are guilty of operating on this misconception when we expect our students to remember something just because we announced it in class. Our supervisor is guilty of operating on this misconception when he or she sends us a memo and expects us to remember to do something.

As we noted in the previous chapter, *encoding* (saying, telling) is just the beginning of the communication process. People who have the "telling is communicating" misconception fail to acknowledge the active role receivers play in the communication process.

Students are not sponges. They hear or read our messages, interpret them, evaluate them in light of their own experiences and needs, and record in their memories what our messages mean to them, if anything. These meanings may be very different from, or even diametrically opposed to, the meanings we intended them to record.

Meaning is the critical variable. Telling does not take into account that the meaning a student assigns to a teacher's messages is determined by the student's background and experiences. In writing this book, for example, it is necessary for us to take into consideration that most teachers have little technical knowledge about human communication theory, but they have much practical experience in actually communicating with other people. Thus, we need to encode and structure the information we hope to communicate (the content of the book) in ways that are consistent with the background and experiences of teachers. If we were to write this book for communication theory specialists, of course, it would need to be written very differently, since the background and experiences of the intended readers would be very different.

Telling is only half of communicating, at best. We must involve our students in the communication process if we hope to help them meet the learning objectives we have set for them.

Misconception Four: Communication Will Solve All Our Problems

At one time or another, each of us has been told by someone that to solve a problem with someone else, all we need to do is communicate with her or him. Communication is viewed by many people in contemporary society as the sure cure, the magic potion, for whatever ails us. Whether we face a problem with our significant other, our principal, a student, or a parent, or whether our country faces a problem with another country, the solution the "experts" are sure to advance is "communication." So-called management consultants sometimes give business executives the impression that if they would just open up lines of communication with subordinates and workers, production and profits would increase steadily. Some counselors suggest that if teachers and parents would just try to communicate more with their children, all manner of problems could be overcome or avoided, including such serious social concerns as drug use and premarital sex. Would that it were so!

Communication can either create or help solve problems. People who view communication as a panacea fail to recognize that what is communicated is far more important than whether communication occurs. As much as our communication efforts may be positively motivated, when we suggest to our male student that he would look far better if he did not wear an earring in his ear, what we are most likely to communicate is that we are a meddling know-nothing who cannot be trusted and should be avoided as much as possible. Has this solved a problem? Hardly; it has created one, possibly many. Should you tell your principal that her or his nose is too big? You decide—and be prepared to reap all the rewards from taking that approach!

Sometimes problems exist that are not amenable to solution, at least in the immediate future. People sometimes have irreconcilable differences, including people who happen to be teachers or students. When such differences occur, it should be recognized that communication offers no guarantee of a solution. Actually, communication may simply stir up the issues even more and make the problem much worse. When you are involved in a conflict with a student, or when you are confronted with students in conflict with one another, the best advice is to get those involved to stop communicating, at least until each person has time to let her or his emotions cool down. Communication during the heat of a conflict increases the conflict; it does not resolve it.

Of course, communication can help us resolve or avoid some problems under some circumstances. We must recognize, however, that communication also can create new problems and make old ones worse. We must be careful what we communicate and when we do it.

Misconception Five: Communication Is a Good Thing

This misconception is pervasive in our society. Ask a politician, a leader in the community, a public administrator. Most will readily espouse the virtues of communication. This misconception probably has its origins in some of the other misconceptions. If you think communication is a panacea for the world's problems, it would seem to follow that communication must be a good thing.

The problem with this thinking is that it places a value on communication in and of itself. *Communication is not good, nor is communication bad. Communication is a tool.* Like any other tool, communication can be used for good or for bad outcomes. By analogy, communication is like many drugs. Used properly, the drug may save our lives. Used improperly, it may kill us. Regardless of one's attitude toward gun control, its opponents make a good point when they use the slogan, "Guns don't kill people, people kill people." Their point is that the tool itself, the gun, is amoral. It is the *use* to which it is put that determines its goodness or badness. One should not forget that one of the most skilled users of communication in the twentieth century was Adolf Hitler. One should not condemn all communication because Hitler used it skillfully, nor should we assume that communication is inherently good because positive outcomes sometimes come as a result of it. As we have indicated previously, simply getting people to communicate with one another does not necessarily mean that good things will occur as a result. Before someone punches another person in the nose, the two people almost always communicate with each other!

Misconception Six: The More Communication, the Better

As we will note in later chapters, the more a person talks (up to a point, at least), the more positively the person will be viewed by others. Research has indicated that talkative people are perceived to be more competent, more friendly, more attractive, more powerful, and better leaders than less talkative people. In mainstream U.S. culture, the prevailing view is that people who talk more are better people.

Of course, we all know people who "talk too much." Actually, it usually isn't how much they talk that causes us to perceive their behavior in this way; it is what they say and how they say it, or when they say it, that causes us to be displeased with them. It is an issue of quality, not quantity. We need to replace this conception with an understanding that *when it comes to communication, quality is more important than quantity.*

The more-is-better misconception leads to many problems in schools. Sometimes the impact is on teachers, who may be bombarded with information from well-meaning, more-is-better administrators. They may feel they are being buried in paper. Too many messages can lead to what is known as "communication overload." When teachers receive more messages than they can handle, they often are unable to sort out what is important from what is unimportant. Hence, the tendency is to ignore most of the messages received.

Would that teachers were the only ones overwhelmed with too many messages! Unfortunately, students, too, are likely to be bombarded by their teachers with more information than they can possibly handle. Students, like other people, have limits on how much communication they can deal with. They often receive a lot of input from their parents, more from their siblings, and more still from their peers. Then they are confronted by enormous amounts from their teachers. Something has to give, and frequently it is the student's capacity to learn. Teachers often cannot resist trying to "get it all covered," whether the "all" is the unit for the week, the book for the course, or whatever. Overload leads to chaotic choices of what messages will be processed or retained. Thus, the more-is-better misconception can lead to more communication but less learning. It would be far better for teachers to recognize that the quality of their communication with students is the real concern, not the quantity.

Misconception Seven: Communication Can Break Down

When people or even nations attempt to influence one another but are unsuccessful, they often feel a need to place blame for that failure. When teachers or students are unsuccessful in communicating, they have a similar need for assigning blame. Not to do so may make it look like they are accepting the failure as their own fault! When they don't, or can't, blame one another, a "communication breakdown" is often identified as the culprit. Somehow, it seems, if we can assert that communication broke down, there will be no need to assume that anyone is at fault.

The concept of "communication breakdown" should be recognized for just what it is: a cop-out intended to cover someone's failure to communicate effectively. When people use the "breakdown" terminology, they usually are suggesting that communication was unsuccessful and has been terminated. In most cases, however, neither of these things has occurred. Often, the communication has been highly successful. The two people fully understand each other; they just do not agree. One may have tried to change the other's mind and failed, but communication did occur. While the two people may have stopped talking to each other, that does not necessarily mean that communication has stopped. The absence of talk often communicates more than talking itself.

It has been observed that *"one cannot not communicate."* The awkwardness of the grammar may make an English teacher wince, but there is real sense in this statement. At least under circumstances where people remain in the same general environment, communication between them will continue, even if talking does not. Avoidance itself sends a message, sometimes a very powerful one. When a man told his spouse that he really did not like her spaghetti, she said nothing. But they did not have a breakdown in communication. Rather, the absence of a single word from her for three days continued the communication. There was no communication breakdown; he just blew it. She did not fail to communicate by not talking. Rather, she really got her point across. And he never, never mentioned anything to her about his evaluation of her meatloaf.

Misconception Eight: Communication Competence Equals Communication Effectiveness

Effectiveness and *competence* are two words that are in the working vocabularies of most English-speaking adults. In many cases, the words can be used interchangeably. Students of language and communication development, however, have learned that such usage often leads people to serious misconceptions about the learning of language and communication skills. It is important to make clear at the outset why this is a misconception.

"Competence" has to do with understanding the communication process. "Effectiveness" has to do with accomplishing what one wants to accomplish through communication. Although the two are related (increasing one's competence increases one's chances of being effective), they are not the same thing. A person who is competent may still not be effective, and a person (for example, a small child) may be effective but not understand why he or she is effective.

Competence relates primarily to cognitive understanding. A child may know the difference between two small animals, such as a cat and a skunk, but may be unable to communicate that to an adult. If, however, the child is asked to point to a picture of either animal, he or she may have no problem doing so. What children know often exceeds what they can communicate effectively.

When we move beyond language development, the distinction between competence and effectiveness grows even more important. To illustrate this, we will consider a somewhat mundane example (McCroskey, 1982). Imagine, if you will, Tom and Bill, two hopelessly incompetent communicators who go together to purchase a bucket of fried chicken at a fast-food restaurant. After a few minutes, the two find that the bucket has one piece of chicken left. Both individuals want the last piece. Words and gestures are exchanged. Tom gets the piece of chicken; Bill does not. If we consider competence to equal effectiveness, we might characterize Tom as "competent," since he was effective in getting the last piece of chicken.

Now imagine that Tom and Bill are two extremely competent communicators. There is one piece of chicken in the bucket, and both individuals want it. They talk for a moment. Bill gets the chicken; Tom does not. Does this now mean that Bill is competent and Tom is not? After all, Tom was not effective in getting the chicken!

As you can see, effectiveness is fairly easily determined by observing a person's behavior. Competence is not so easily determined. Competence has to do with knowing what needs to be done. Effectiveness has to do with outcomes. Knowing how to do something right, even doing it right, does not guarantee that desired outcomes will occur. Even the best bowler does not make a strike every time. By contrast, chance may produce a desired result even in the absence of any real competence. Sometimes the beginning bowler simply drops the ball on the alley, but the bowler still gets a strike.

Some beginning teachers are like beginning bowlers. They may have no idea what they are doing but may still get something positive accomplished. Of course, the odds are strongly against such an outcome. After all, most beginning bowlers throw the ball in the gutter unless they have had careful instruction before they make their first attempt. Even then, they may need quite a bit of practice before they regularly get it right.

Competence and effectiveness are not the same thing. Reading this book should help you build your level of competence. But until you practice some of the things you learn, your effectiveness as a classroom communicator is not likely to improve.

One of the major barriers to learning about the role of communication in the classroom is having misconceptions about the process of communication. These misconceptions make it difficult to understand how communication really works. This chapter has been devoted to confronting some of the most common misconceptions. We hope that you now understand both why people have these misconceptions and some of the alternative conceptions that are available and that can provide you with a more solid base for understanding instructional communication.

References

Hurt, H. T., Scott, M. D., & McCroskey, J. C. (1978). *Communication in the classroom*. Reading, MA: Addison-Wesley.

McCroskey, J. C. (1982). Communication competence and performance: A research and pedagogical perspective. *Communication Education, 31,* 1–8.

McCroskey, J. C. (2006). *An introduction to rhetorical communication*, 9th ed. Boston: Allyn & Bacon.

McCroskey, J. C., & Richmond, V. P. (1995). *Fundamentals of human communication: An interpersonal perspective*. Prospect Heights, IL: Waveland.

McCroskey, J. C., & Wheeless, L. R. (1976). *Introduction to human communication*. Boston: Allyn & Bacon.

Glossary

conception   A way of thinking about and/or understanding something.

meanings   Ideas and conceptualizations that exist in people's minds.

nonverbal communication   The process by which one person (or group) stimulates meaning in the mind of another (or others) through the use of nonverbal messages.

telling   The process of sending a message to another person or persons.

verbal communication   The process by which one person (or group) stimulates meaning in the mind of another (or others) through use of oral and/or written language (messages).

words   Codes or symbols for meanings that people have in their minds.

3

Getting Started

A sizable portion of a teacher's total communication experience in a given day is initiated by someone else—students, other teachers, supervisors, parents, and so on. Frequently, we have little choice about whether or not to communicate. Someone comes into our classroom and asks us a question. We are mandated to communicate in return, even if all we do is turn away and say nothing. Such a refusal to engage in verbal communication will certainly communicate, and in a very negative way! As we noted in the previous chapter, we cannot *not* communicate in such circumstances. Nevertheless, we do exert considerable control over the extent to which we communicate. In some instances we may choose to initiate communication, and in other instances we may choose not to. Our concern here is why we choose to in some cases and not in others.

Communication Motivations

Our perception of our communication choices is normally based on our projection of the probable outcomes of communicating or not communicating in the given instance. If we predict the outcome will be to our advantage, we will probably choose to communicate. If our projection is negative, of course, we will probably try to avoid communication. The outcomes with which teachers are most likely to be concerned include developing and maintaining affinity, acquiring information or understanding, influencing others, reaching decisions, confirming beliefs, and expressing feelings. Although it may come as a surprise to some, the outcomes of primary concern to students are the same as those of concern to teachers.

Developing and Maintaining Affinity

"Affinity" is liking, being attracted to, or wanting to be near some other person. Gaining affinity from another person, or maintaining such affinity, is often a desired outcome of communication. Most people have a need for warm relationships with other people. We do not want to be rejected or become isolated from other human beings. Although there are some exceptions, the overwhelming majority of both teachers and students have a very high desire to gain affinity from each other. It may be that some teachers do not care if their students like them or not, but most know that their lives will be much more pleasant if their students have a high regard for them. Similarly, while it may be "cool" for students to tell other students they don't care what teachers think of them, most know that if the teacher likes them, their world will be a much more pleasant place.

These general predispositions may be the norm, but it is important to recognize that there is considerable variability among both teachers and students. Thus, although much of both teachers' and students' initiation of communication comes as a result of a desire to gain affinity with others, some have a stronger desire to do so, and some have a much weaker desire.

Students who have a very high need for affinity often strive to become the "teacher's pet." They sometimes try too hard to please, are agreeable to almost anything the teacher wants, and may always seem to be underfoot. Such behavior is usually observed and recognized by other students before it is recognized by the teacher, since positive attention is desired by most teachers, and it is nice to think it is deserved. Similarly, teachers with an unusually high need for affinity go out of their way to be nice to their students and avoid doing things that might put themselves in a less positive light. For instance, they might avoid assigning homework, dole out few tests, assign high grades, excuse inappropriate behavior, and so on. These teacher behaviors are likely to be noticed first by other teachers or by supervisors than by students . Sometimes the teacher is not even aware he or she is engaging in these unprofessional behaviors. Of course, the supervisor may not notice what is going on because the teacher is also actively "kissing up" to her or him.

Students and teachers at the other end of this continuum can create problems, too. Students with a low need for affinity may simply avoid opportunities for communication with peers and teachers. This may cause them to be seen as loners or simply ignored. Some low-affinity students may actively express a dislike for their teachers and peers. Expressions of "negative affinity" may lead to serious conflicts, as most people don't respond well to such behavior.

Teachers with an unusually low need for affinity may be a very disruptive force in a school. They may behave very much as students do who have similar needs. If they simply withdraw, they may be seen by other teachers as not collegial and as not carrying their share of the load. Students are likely to see them as hostile and uncaring. These perceptions often affect the class and the subject matter the teacher is covering and, as a result, have a very negative impact on the student's affective learning.

It has been estimated that between 50 and 90 percent of all interpersonal communication occurs primarily because of the participants' motivation to seek affinity with one another (McCroskey & Wheeless, 1976). Although acquiring information or understanding is presumed to be the primary communication objective in an instructional context, when we look at the entire school context, it is probable that this estimate of the proportion of communication motivated by affinity is accurate in the instructional context as well. Even when other outcomes may be desired in a communication relationship, seldom is affinity completely irrelevant. Even the principal wants to be loved!

Acquiring Information or Understanding

School is about information and understanding. Teachers have it, and students want it. Although both of these statements are very idealistic and not very realistic, they are assumptions we generally accept as the foundation of the school environment. Information—acquiring it and dispensing it—is our business. Indeed, most people, both children and adults, want to learn. If the circumstances are right, they will even go out of their way to initiate communication to do so.

The need for information and understanding is a common motivation for communication. Students may attend class and/or read textbooks because they feel a need for information or understanding. Teachers initiate communication with students so they can better understand those students and be better able to facilitate their learning.

Influencing Others

As human beings, we can control some aspects of our world directly by our own behavioral choices. We may, for example, grow some of our own food. For the most part, however, we must have the cooperation of others if we are to prosper and have much control within our environment. To gain that cooperation, we need to influence others, just as others need to influence us to gain our cooperation. Influence, like cooperation, is a two-way street.

Teachers and students feel the need to influence each other, as well as their own peers. It has been said that there are two ways to influence others: to coerce them or to persuade them. The first option is dependent on the use or threat of force. The second is dependent on communication. Most would agree that persuasion is the preferred method in an instructional environment, although the alternative method is sometimes employed.

The idealist may believe that students are always motivated to learn, but the realist recognizes that teachers need to encourage that motivation in many cases. At the university level, it may be enough to simply present information and let students decide whether to learn it or ignore it, but it is certainly is not enough at earlier levels of instruction. Even at the university level, teachers who are recognized as excellent are almost always the ones who influence their students to want to learn from them. Teachers at the elementary and secondary levels are destined to be failures if they ignore the need to influence their students' behaviors.

Although we noted earlier that most people think school is about information, that really is not the case. Societies do not tax their people to create schools just to disseminate information. Schools are designed to perpetuate the culture of the people who support them. This is done by influencing the beliefs, attitudes, values, and (most important) the behaviors of the students—not just while they are in school but also long after their schooling is completed. Thus, from a community perspective, the role of the teacher is primarily to be an influence agent. Much of the communication initiated by teachers is specifically directed toward influencing the thoughts, feelings, and behaviors of their students.

Reaching Decisions

Although decision making is a major reason for communication in many environments, it is not a particularly significant factor in the classroom. It's true that teachers must communicate with other teachers and supervisors to make many instructional decisions, and students need to communicate with others to make many of the decisions in their lives, but teachers and students in a classroom setting do not normally engage in much communication directed toward reaching decisions. Where this occurs, it is usually in specialized instructional contexts that involve a lot of individualized attention.

Confirming Beliefs

After we make a decision or draw a conclusion, it is common to talk to others to confirm we have decided wisely. When we choose from a variety of alternatives, particularly when there seem to be several good options, we are often disturbed by having had to reject one alternative to accept another. Consider having to decide whether to take a position that would provide a substantial increase in salary or to take one that would provide more free time to be with family.

Whichever option is chosen, it is likely that the road not taken will continue to be attractive, maybe even more so than before we made the decision. This kind of psychological stress is sometimes known as "dissonance." To reduce it, we often communicate with other people to confirm that they would have made the same choice we did had they been in our place, or to gain information that will make our choice seem more desirable and the alternative choices less desirable. We often see this type of behavior in students who have elective choices for classes to take. It is very important to them to feel that they have chosen the right courses. They may be overheard praising a class they chose to take, but at the same time, they may be condemning a required course, since they have no emotional stake in that class. Teachers will behave similarly, only the choices are different.

Expressing Feelings

In Chapter 1, we distinguished between expressive and other types of communication. As we noted, expressive communication arises from the feelings or emotions of the individual. This type of communication is personality driven. Another person with the same feelings might not express them at all. Some people have a very high need to express whatever they feel. Others are very private. No matter what they might be feeling, those around them are unlikely to know about it.

Both students and teachers may initiate communication to express their feelings, but it is more common for students to do this than for teachers. Small children often exude the need to express themselves. They may not even care whether anyone else hears them at all. They will express their feelings even if no one else is present. As we grow older, most of us learn that we need to control the external expressions of our feelings and emotions. However, that does not necessarily reduce our desire to express them. Part of having a close relationship with another person is knowing that we can convey our feelings to that person without being judged. Acknowledgment is often the only response required.

Because many students do not have such close relationships, it is not unusual for them to try to develop a substitute relationship with a teacher. When this happens, it is important for the teacher to be accepting of the student so that he or she can vent built-up feelings. Teachers should also recognize that there's no need to judge or respond to those expressive messages beyond acknowledging that they have been heard.

When teachers regularly find it necessary to express their emotions and feelings to a class full of students, it may create a serious problem. Mature adults are expected to find a more appropriate outlet for communicating their feelings. Students are unlikely to know how to respond. They may question the stability and/or motives of the teacher. Some may want to stay away from that teacher because they think he or she is "weird." Teachers must control the expression of their feelings in their classrooms.

Choice of Communication Partners

As we have noted, there are a variety of reasons why people choose to communicate. Usually, communication is designed to meet the individual needs of the person initiating the communication. We turn our attention now to why someone chooses a particular person with whom to initiate communication. Such choices are far from random. We will consider five reasons here.

Proximity

Before we start looking for more surprising reasons why people choose certain others with whom to communicate, we certainly should consider the obvious, although when people are asked to come up with reasons why they talk to certain people and not to others, this "obvious" explanation often is not mentioned. People communicate most with people who are around them most.

If you can recover from the shock of this revelation, let us continue; actual research has been conducted in this area, and the results are interesting. After four years of studying 25,000 pairs of college students, Priest and Sawyer (1967) concluded that such communicative pairs are most likely to form in order of increasing proximity. That is, college roommates were the most likely to pair, then students living in different rooms on the same floor, then students on different floors of the same building, and then students living in different buildings.

Think of the person with whom you talk most every day. It might be your spouse, your child, or one of your parents. It also might be a teacher in the classroom next to yours. It might be the person with whom you ride back and forth to work. Now recall that good friend you talked with virtually every day back in high school. When was the last time you spoke with that person? If you no longer live close to where you went to high school, or if that good friend does not live near you, the odds are that you have not talked to that person in years! Is proximity all your friendship was based on? Not really, but that was a critical part of it. Research indicates that unless other factors are very strong, as proximity decreases, so does communication. If someone moves away, you may try to maintain contact for a while, but as time passes, those efforts will decrease. Over time, the communication may terminate completely.

Why do children talk to those who sit next to them in class? Because they are there. No matter how much the teacher moves children around to get them to stop talking to each other, he or she is fighting a losing battle. Proximity is the first factor influencing a child's choice of communication targets. Seating a different child in the same proximate relationship will, at best, serve as only a temporary solution. This is one of those battles that is not worth fighting, for the teacher will lose one way or another. He or she will only alienate students by taking on the battle. Winning the battle can only mean stifling virtually all communication in the classroom, and that will do far more harm than good.

Attraction

People communicate more with those whom they find to be attractive than with those they find to be unattractive. We are not only talking about physical attraction, although that certainly is a critical factor for all of us from puberty on. As we will discuss in greater detail in Chapter 6, there are three dimensions of interpersonal attraction: physical, social, and task. Simply defined: Does the person look good? Do we want to socialize with the person? Do we want to work with the person? If the answer to any one of these questions is yes, the probability is greater that we will seek to communicate with her or him.

The physical attractiveness factor becomes particularly noticeable in the upper-elementary and high school years. Boys are chasing girls, and girls are chasing boys. The desire to communicate about school decreases as other desires become more relevant.

Homophily

Literally, *homophily* refers to two living things coming from the same category. Two leaves from walnut trees, two collie dogs, two cities in northern Minnesota, or two people from Beckley, West Virginia, may be said to have homophily. In the field of communication, *homophily* is commonly used to reference two people who are distinctly similar in one or more ways.

The principle of homophily, in part, suggests that the more similar two communicators are, the more likely they are to interact with each other. This is an extension of the old saying that "like attracts like." People with similar background and/or attitudes tend to form groups in which they do most of their communicating. Often, demographic similarities are sufficient for people to group themselves together for communication. Age, sex, race, and religion are powerful factors that can cause people to group together. No matter how much we as a society believe in equality, it remains far more likely that an Irish, Catholic, sixteen-year-old female will talk with someone who is demographically similar than it is that she will talk to a Japanese, Buddhist, fifty-seven-year-old male.

People choose to communicate with those who are like themselves because they believe they will have a better understanding of where that other person is coming from. People do not like uncomfortable interactions. Thus, if they confront a person who is clearly not like themselves, they are likely to avoid initiating interaction for fear that such discomfort might arise. This will not always be the case, for sometimes people actively seek to communicate with those who are very different from themselves to better understand other types of people. Nevertheless, initiation of such risky interactions remains a comparatively rare event.

Utility

Communication is necessary to satisfy most human needs. Hence, people choose to communicate with those who are in a position to help them meet their needs. We ask a clerk about how a product works because we don't want to buy it and then find we can't make it function. We stop in a convenience store to ask directions to where we are going so we won't get lost. Teachers ask the principal or the office staff how to interpret a rule so they can follow it. Students ask the teacher to explain a concept so they can understand and learn it. In short, we "use" others through our communication with them to satisfy our needs.

Loneliness or Frustration

Sometimes people reach out to communicate with others simply because they are lonely or frustrated by an absence of human contact. Although this factor may overlap somewhat with general "utility," which we just discussed, the need here is one for human interaction and companionship, not the utilitarian need for help from someone else through communication. When a person is lonely or frustrated, the communication itself is what is needed.

While some people— people often called "loners" or "hermits"—have little or no need or desire to interact with others, most people have a strong desire for human interaction. They have a need for "phatic" communication, if nothing else. Phatic communication is essentially talk for its own sake. Much of the communication in which we participate daily is of this type. Our greeting and goodbye rituals are examples of such talk. It is our way of acknowledging others without getting involved with them. When someone talks to us, it ratifies our existence. It shows that somebody cares, if only a little!

If such contact is not a regular part of a person's daily experience, he or she may need to reach out to obtain that contact from almost anyone. For instance, homemakers who spend all day with a small child for days on end often feel that what they need most is a chance to interact with another adult human being. If they do not obtain enough of that interaction from a spouse, they may take every opportunity available to interact with neighbors, delivery persons, salespersons, or anyone else who wanders into their path.

Loneliness is a powerful motivation for communication. Some students, even though they are around other students all day, have little or no interaction with these other students. They may be lonely because they are not conventionally attractive, because they come from a different demographic background, or because they receive little attention at home. Just like everyone else, these students have a need to interact with someone, virtually anyone. Often, these individuals will choose to initiate communication with a teacher. The interaction may be strained, and the teacher may not be able to understand why the student is taking up her or his time, but the interaction may be very important to the student. In fact, it may be virtually all the communicative contact he or she has in a day.

As we have seen, there are many reasons why people need to communicate. Children and students of all ages are, first of all, people. Thus, they experience the need to communicate, just like other people. And, lest we forget, so do teachers!

The Acquaintance Process

Whenever we come into contact with another person and anticipate that this contact will be continued into the future (as opposed to brief contact with a sales clerk or the like), we enter into the acquaintance process. Through this process, we presume we will "get to know" the other individual. This may or may not actually happen. To better understand how this special communication context functions, or fails to function, let's examine how it normally takes place.

One of the first things that normally happens when we come into contact with a new person is that we introduce ourselves to each other. Sometimes this is initiated by a third party who knows both people. Sometimes one person knows who the other is and so only needs to introduce herself or himself. The initial interaction is normally restricted to such subjects as name, occupation, and where both people come from and/or live. Marital status and number of children may be discussed, although these are not always considered appropriate topics. More likely subjects are the weather and recent or upcoming sporting events in the area or on television.

Few initial interactions go further than this, and most do not even go this far. Depending on the extent of subsequent contact, this may be the only communication the two people have for the rest of their lives, even if they are neighbors or work near each other. Nevertheless, if someone were to ask either one of these individuals whether they "know" the other, an affirmative response would be likely.

We don't really know most of the people we are quite willing to say we know. However, if we continue our interaction with a person substantially beyond this initial level, we are likely to get to know her or him much better. At the outset, topics of an intimate or personal nature are taboo, as they carry a high risk of offense. What would you think if a person you just met asked you what your sexual preferences were or if you had ever been fired from a job? Or, short of that, suppose the other person related to you her or his own sexual preferences or informed you that she or he had been fired last week? Such topics may never be appropriate, but certainly not in initial interactions.

As we interact with a person at greater length over an extended period of time, we may begin to share opinions about a variety of topics concerning work, hobbies, social interests, and the like. After a while, we may even engage in some discussion of religious or political views, but discussion of these topics is likely to terminate the relationship if begun too soon.

Only a very few of our relationships will mature and develop to the stage where communication about intimate topics would be considered appropriate. Thus, although we are generally not aware of it, most of us really "know" very few people. While the great majority of our communication is with the few people we know well, most of the individuals with whom we interact are, for all intents and purposes, strangers. Even if we have met them, we do not know them well enough to talk about serious matters with them. But sometimes, we must.

A basic principle of effective communication is that we need to adapt our messages to the person with whom we are communicating. Hence, as we meet and interact with another person, we are trying to understand what makes her or him "tick." We are seeking to understand the person's attitudes, beliefs, and values, her or his biases, philosophies, and unique experiences. We are trying to predict how the person will respond to our messages before we send them.

Because most of our interactions with people happen at a very superficial level, making good predictions is very difficult. We may be as likely to be wrong about how someone will react to what we say as we are to be right, or even more so. This can pose serious problems when it comes to communication in the classroom. To examine this, we need to explore the levels at which people can communicate.

Levels of Communication

The three levels of communication that are commonly identified in books on interpersonal communication are cultural, sociological, and psychological. Since much of the communication that happens in the instructional arena is of an interpersonal nature, this classification scheme is useful for our purposes.

Cultural

The *cultural level* refers to what we know about people in large national or regional groups. At this level, we make predictions and interact using the kind of information we obtain in our normal interaction with someone, as we just described. This is the level at which the mass media must communicate the vast majority of the time. Little is known about the individual who is receiving the message, so stereotypes of how such people generally would react must be used to make the predictions we use for adaptation.

Note that we are not using the term *stereotype* in a derogatory fashion here. Stereotypes are simply generalizations based on incomplete information. They are derived from whatever general information is available about the group to which a person appears to belong. That information may be accurate for a very large portion of that group or for only a very small portion. Hence, the stereotype may be accurate for the person we are trying to communicate with, but it may not be. Conclusions based on stereotypes are very likely to be wrong—hence the negative associations attached to the idea of "stereotyping." However, we all must base our communication predictions on such stereotypes until we have sufficient information to draw better conclusions. If all the information we have is a person's ethnic background, age, and sex, we may know that that is not enough to guarantee good predictions, but nevertheless, we must still make predictions. It should come as no surprise, therefore, that most thinking people want to limit their interaction with others to "safe" topics until they know more about the person with whom they are communicating.

Sociological

When we communicate at the *sociological level*, we base our predictions about the other person not only on cultural-level information but also on information about the groups to which he or she belongs. Important information can be gleaned from knowledge about a person's occupational group, political or religious affiliation, membership in social or service clubs, economic group, and so on. Although such information provides a far less than perfect basis for making predictions about a person's beliefs, attitudes, and values, it is better than simply knowing that the person is a twenty-seven-year-old male Caucasian.

Although there is substantial variation in the orientations of individuals within any given group, people tend to come together in groups because of their similarities. As a result, stereotypes based on group affiliation and cultural variables are more likely to be accurate than those based on cultural variables alone. To know, for example, that a young woman is an active member of the National Organization for Women (NOW) will probably give us a fairly good picture of her attitudes on a number of current political issues. Similarly, if we know she is also a member of the chamber of commerce in her city, that information would indicate that she might feel strongly about some local concerns. It is vital to remember, however, that not all members of NOW or the chamber of commerce think alike. It is just that a guess based on such cues has more likelihood of being right than it would be without the information. It still can be wrong.

Psychological

Communication at the *psychological level* involves making predictions based on knowledge of the other person as an individual rather than just as a member of a group or a culture. Conclusions drawn about how the person is most likely to act in a given situation, while still stereotypes, have a much greater likelihood of being accurate. This information is drawn from the individuals communicating with one another over time and feeds back into the communication of the individuals by reducing the number and seriousness of errors in prediction that people make.

Clearly, it is preferable to be able to communicate with another person at the psychological level. Doing so lets us adapt messages to the person more accurately and greatly increases the likelihood of effective communication. Unfortunately, most of us know very few people well enough to communicate with them at this level. Most people with whom we come into contact in our day-to-day lives must be dealt with only at a cultural or sociological level; we have no other choice.

When we enter the instructional arena, we find ourselves in a bit of a quandary. The highest probability we have for successfully communicating with students and hence enhancing their learning to the maximum degree possible occurs when a teacher is able to adapt to the personality of the individual student. But the reality is that teachers at most levels have so many students, they hardly know them as individuals at all.

Out of economic necessity, much of the education that takes place at the secondary and university levels must operate at the cultural level or, at best, the sociological level. It really is mass communication, not interpersonal communication. Messages must be developed by textbook writers, curriculum specialists, and individual teachers based on predictions made about learners in general. As we write this book, we are adapting to each reader via our stereotype of the "typical teacher." The fact that we have worked with thousands of elementary and secondary school teachers in our careers gives us a richer and more well-rounded stereotype to work with than someone who has had less such contact, but it is not as if we know *you!*

In spite of the fact that educators know an enormous amount about differences in students' learning styles, most instructional materials are not adapted to the learning styles of particular students. To do so would be almost impossible. Thus, in instructional communication, it is left to the individual teacher to adapt to the individual student. That is a tall order for the college instructor when a university course may enroll more than a thousand students, with more than two hundred in any section of the course. It is not much less difficult for the secondary school teacher who has five or six classes with thirty to forty students in each class. Let us not forget how challenging it is for the kindergarten teacher to adapt to twenty virtually unsocialized little ones running all over the room at once.

We must face up to the fact that most of the time we are not going to reach the desired psychological communication level when communicating with our students. In fact, our students will actually have less difficulty adapting to us than we will to them. After all, each one of them has only a few of us with whom to cope! The more sophisticated students (not necessarily older; some second graders are quite sophisticated in this way) will be able to adapt to us, so as to enhance our communication with them.

Although we may never reach the ideal level of communication with every student, we can improve our communicative relationship with many of them. We can do this by simply recognizing that students communicate with the same motivations and limitations that we do. They are people, just as teachers are people. If teachers are willing to accept that fact and treat the students that way, the communication between teachers and students will be greatly enhanced. It will not be perfect, but, fortunately, it does not have to be.

References

McCroskey, J. C., & Richmond, V. P. (1995). *Fundamentals of human communication: An interpersonal perspective.* Prospect Heights, IL: Waveland.

McCroskey, J. C., & Wheeless, L. R. (1976). *Introduction to human communication.* Boston: Allyn & Bacon.

Priest, R. F., & Sawyer, J. (1967). Proximity and peership: Bases of balance in interpersonal attraction. *American Journal of Sociology, 72,* 633–649.

Glossary

affinity   Liking, being attracted to, and/or wanting to be near some other person.

attraction   The degree to which a person wants to be with, and communicate with, another person.

communication motivations   The reasons why a person chooses to communicate or not to communicate.

homophily   The degree to which a person sees another person as being similar to her- or himself.

influence   The state of altering another person's attitudes, beliefs, values, or behaviors.

level of communication   Representation of the depth of knowledge people have about one another. The cultural level indicates little knowledge; the sociological level indicates moderate knowledge; and the psychological level indicates much knowledge.

principle of homophily   The more similar two people are, the more likely they will attempt to communicate with each other, the more likely that communication will be successful, and the more alike the two people will become.

proximity   The degree of physical, or psychological, distance between people.

4

Common Classroom Communication Problems

There are certain problems that are likely to be found in virtually all instructional systems that involve communication between teachers or trainers and students. Before we move on to some of the larger communication issues, it is useful to look at some of these everyday dilemmas. These concerns often underlie what appear to be much larger issues, and overcoming problems at this level often leads to discovering solutions to other problems as well. In this chapter we'll look at some of the things that can go wrong so that communication between teacher or trainer and student is less effective than it can and should be.

Quietness

Quietness can be a problem for the instructor, for the student, or both. It can be a problem introduced by the principal or administrator. Regardless of where it comes from, it needs to be identified and dealt with.

For many, the image of the ideal classroom is one where learners are seated in neat rows facing the instructor, who is talking or writing on the chalkboard. Anyone who has taught in or even visited a real school knows that image has nothing to do with reality. Even if the administration insists on rigid regimentation of the students, this idealized image of the classroom atmosphere is unlikely to be achieved. If it were, the amount of learning that would occur in such a classroom would likely be less than that which occurs at present in the average classroom.

Quietness is not central to a good learning environment. This is not to say that students screaming at the top of their lungs, running all around the room, throwing things at one another, and jumping on desks is preferable. Too often people think these are the only two options available. Fortunately, that is not the case.

Within the U.S. system of education, particularly at the lower levels of instruction, talking is seen as very important. This is not true for educational systems everywhere in the world or even in many training programs in U.S. organizations. For example, after visiting several U.S. schools, an acquaintance of ours who teaches at a university in Sweden made the following comment: "You Americans have a peculiar view of how children learn. We Swedes believe children learn through their eyes and ears. You seem to believe children learn through their mouths."

When put that way, it gives one pause and may even make one reexamine one's views on how children should be taught. Such a reexamination will bring most people right back where they were. Children really do learn as a function of talking, and the talking has other benefits as well. There are several facts that support this conclusion.

1. *Student talk usually is learning related.* Certainly, some student-to-student talk has nothing to do with what is being taught. High school students may be making dates or planning other after-school social activities. Elementary school students may be teasing one another or sharing gossip. These are the kinds of things teachers frequently believe are going on when they see students talking to one another. This kind of talk behavior, however, is not the norm in most classrooms. It is much more likely that one student is asking another for help, giving an example of what the teacher was just talking about, or relating what is being taught to something else the two students know about.

2. *Students need to talk to overcome confusion or misunderstanding.* Sometimes student talk happens because a student didn't hear a point that the teacher was trying to make. Students depend more on their peers to explain ideas than they do on teachers. Many students feel uncomfortable asking teachers questions. If they cannot ask another student, they may never get the concept clarified. Besides, peers often are better able to explain concepts to one another in language that they understand than teachers are.

3. *Students need to talk and move to relieve tension and stress.* Learning is a stressful activity, particularly for young children. For this reason, recess or some other regularly permitted free time is vital for students. They need to be allowed to "let off steam." A teacher's insensitivity to this need may cause severe problems in the classroom. If the student cannot relieve tension one way, he or she will do so in another way. Often such a release will come in the form of classroom disruption. As children grow older, such breaks are needed somewhat less frequently, but the need never disappears completely. Thus, if high school students are not permitted to talk to one another between classes in the hallways, they are much more likely to talk socially in the classroom instead of listening to the teacher.

4. *Children learn communication by communicating.* Communication skills are inadequately taught both in the home and in school. Hence, children must learn most of their communication skills through trial and error. If children are told to be quiet at home, to be quiet on the bus, and to be quiet everywhere in school, where are they supposed to practice communicating? The answer is that many don't get that practice, and their communicative development is slowed as a result.

Sometimes it is not the school, the teacher, or the parent that is pushing the student to be quiet. Such pressure can come from within the student as a part of her or his personality. We will consider this basis for quietness in Chapters 10 and 11.

Class and Group Size

That class size affects the nature of communication in classrooms should come as no surprise to anyone who has gone to school, much less taught a variety of different-sized classes. Indeed, the size of any group has an effect on the communication that occurs between people within it. Here we will consider a few of the effects that may have an impact on both communication and learning.

1. *As size increases, attention to any one member decreases.* There is only so much attention to go around. Thus, the more people there are in a class, the less attention a teacher can give to any one student. Consequently, the teacher will obtain less psychological-level data about each student and is less able to adapt communication to each individual. The result, of course, is a reduction in individualization in instruction. Predictions made about individual students in this scenario must be drawn from a baser level of stereotype and are more likely to be in error. Reduced learning on the part of each student should be expected.

Based on this analysis, then, we can conclude that the more students there are in a class, the less learning will be achieved, right? Not necessarily. It depends on how you calculate the amount of learning. If you have 100 students and each student achieves 50 units of learning, the total learning in the class would be 5,000 units. If you reduce class size to 25 students, and each student learns twice as much, or 100 units, the total learning in the class is 2,500 units. The smaller class produces either half as much learning or twice as much learning, depending on how you count! Both communication and economics must be considered in deciding what class size is optimal.

2. *As size increases, average amount of talking decreases.* There is only so much talk-time available. As more people become involved in the class, the amount of talk-time that can be devoted to each individual must necessarily decrease. If talking is indeed important to learning, as we suggested earlier in this chapter, increased class size must reduce learning. In larger classes, teachers tend to take up more of the talk-time, in some cases virtually 100 percent of it. While this is not preferred by many students, some will actually learn more in such a course. These are the students who are afraid to speak up in class. In smaller classes, they are constantly worrying about being forced to talk and cannot concentrate on learning what is being taught. In larger classes, they can relax and concentrate on what is being said, knowing that no one will harass them into talking.

3. *Large groups tend to break into small groups.* Subgroups or cliques are often composed of people who are friends outside the larger group context. Students who attend large schools are likely to know fewer students than students who attend small schools. In fact, many students in large schools complain of loneliness and a lack of friends. Teachers need to be attentive to this concern when including group work in their instructional system. If students are allowed to choose their own groups, they will almost always retreat to their cliques, and some students will be hard-pressed to find a group that will accept them. It's much better for the teacher to assign members to groups, so that everyone will be included, and to try to avoid placing students in a clique that is likely to ignore or reject them.

4. *Groups tend to spontaneously generate leaders.* This tendency increases as the size of the group increases. These leaders do not necessarily emerge as a function of the excellence of their leadership skills. More typically, the first person to talk or attempt to exert any kind of influence will become the leader. If the teacher is using group activities to facilitate learning rather than just to fill time, he or she should make certain that serious students are appointed as group leaders. Otherwise, the more verbal students, who are sometimes less than fully motivated toward learning goals, will take charge of the groups.

Rumor and Serial Communication

In Chapter 2, we discussed why communication is not always a good thing. Although people sometimes have a difficult time accepting this idea at first, almost everyone agrees with it as soon as the issue of rumors comes up. Most of us have been the victim of a vicious rumor at one time or another. Not many rumors are intentionally started to hurt someone, although that certainly is possible. Very often, there is some grain of truth in a rumor. After all, something got it started. However, the rumor can grow to a point where it is unrecognizable even to those who started it.

Rumors are subject to the vagaries of serial communication. Serial communication refers to the process of messages being passed from one person to another, on to another, and so on. The steps in the serial process are not naturally limited. However, after only a few steps, the content may be so altered in the process that it is no longer recognizable. Several things happen as information passes through one person to another.

1. *There is too much information.* If you throw six basketballs to someone all at once, it is very unlikely that all six will be caught—even if the person you throw them to is an NBA All-Star. Only so many balls can be caught at once. It is much the same with ideas; people can only cope with so many at once. If too many messages are received in a short period of time, they cannot all be processed and remembered. Some ideas, therefore, will not be recalled when a person tries to pass the information on to someone else.

2. *Some information is seen as unimportant.* Small details, particularly when there is a lot of information, are likely to be seen as unimportant by the person processing the message. Of course, what one person considers a small detail may be seen as critical information by someone else. This is the essence of the plot line in many crime mysteries: Everyone but the hero misses a small but critical bit of information.

Because of these two factors, the second person to receive a message is likely to have a distorted idea of what he or she was told. Some things are just missed, and other things are seen as unimportant. When this person wants to, or is asked to, relate the story to someone else, a jumble of information is recalled. This may lead to four other factors, which may produce the wild rumors we are likely to hear. Let us consider each.

1. *Information may be added to make better sense of the story.* If something is missing that is needed to link two ideas that are clearly recalled, the person telling the story is likely to add something he or she thinks is reasonable so that the story makes more sense. The person may not even be aware that such an addition is being made but may actually believe he or she just temporarily forgot it and then remembered it.

2. *Information may be added to make the story more interesting.* Good storytellers have a flair for making their stories interesting. Small but interest-provoking details are likely to be added, and these interesting bits may grow in subsequent tellings. A jostle may grow into a shove, a shove may grow into a punch, a punch may grow into a fight, a fight may grow into a brawl, and a brawl may grow into a riot. And that is only through five tellings of the story!

3. *Information may be changed to make sense out of it.* If we remember information that does not make sense to us, we will probably suspect we remembered it wrong. If changing a detail causes the rest of the story to make sense, we are likely to think we were initially mistaken and that now we have remembered it correctly. Not only the person telling the story but also the person hearing it is likely to believe the "corrected" version is accurate in the future.

4. *Information may be changed to fit one's biases or expectations.* People often hear what they expect to hear, even if what is said is somewhat different. This is not an intentionally malicious behavior. In fact, when we do this, we may be totally unaware that we are doing it. Nevertheless, both the storyteller and the listener will probably believe the altered version of the information.

At this point, you may be wondering why this is of concern to a person interested in the role of communication in instruction. Communication in instruction is almost always part of a serial communication process. Teachers are seldom the people who generate the information they teach (although that sometimes is the case in research universities). They obtain the information from somewhere

(where it has probably already passed through several steps of the serial process) and pass it along to their students, who may pass it along to their peers or even to their parents. Have you ever been criticized for something you said in class that you are positive you did not say? Ever had a student write out an answer on a test and not been able to imagine whence it might have come? Usually these things are a result of the serial communication process.

While what is happening in this situation is normal, if we permit it to occur in our classroom, the quality of our students' learning will be lowered. To exaggerate only slightly, if we do not help our students overcome the problems of serial communication, what they will learn will be nothing more than rumors. To help, we first need to understand how students actually acquire information.

The Nature of Schemas

Have you ever had the feeling that as you told someone something, it was going in one ear and out the other? At least figuratively, it may have done just that. Why is it that some students can listen to a lecture and come away with information they may retain for the rest of their lives while other students cannot remember anything the lecturer said five minutes after he or she said it? Is it a matter of differences in intelligence? Not really.

People learn by placing information into categories with information that is similar. Category systems of this kind are known as schemas. Imagine that you are in a post office that has mailboxes. The postal clerk invites you to walk around back so you can see the boxes from the other side. What you see is row after row of boxes, all connected to one another. In a small town, these boxes may have people's names marked on them. In a larger city, the boxes are more likely to have numbers. The postal clerk sorts through the mail, puts the pieces in the various boxes, and has some mail left over that does not go into any of the boxes. That mail must be returned, or some other method must be employed to find the person for whom it is intended.

Students' schema systems are somewhat like the mailboxes. As information comes in, it is placed in a "box" if it belongs there. If no box can be found for it, it will be shunted aside to be considered later, or simply ignored. Figure 4.1 gives an example of a very unsophisticated schema system. This might represent a young child's schema for dogs. The child has a basset hound, and the neighbor has a poodle. The child has not seen other dogs. If information comes to the child in the form of pictures of dogs, the hound pictures will go in one category and the poodle

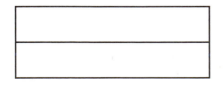

FIGURE 4.1
Unsophisticated
Schema System

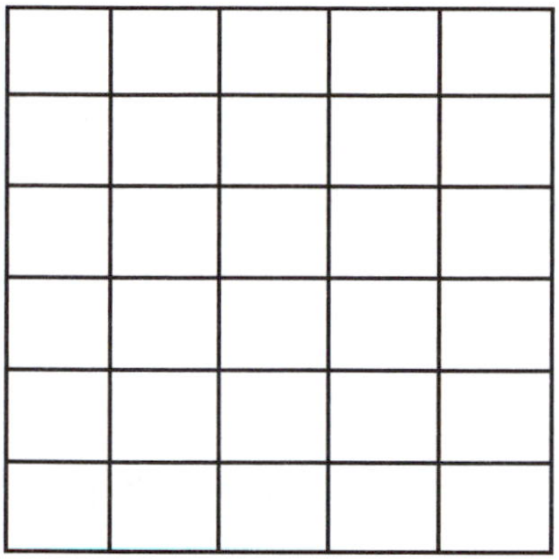

FIGURE 4.2
*Sophisticated Schema
System*

pictures will go in the other. The remaining pictures will either be put in an incorrect box or will just be set aside. As the child gets more and more exposure to dogs, her or his schema for dogs will grow and eventually look more like Figure 4.2, a sophisticated schema system. This book, in large measure, is designed to help you develop your schema for communication in instruction to look less like Figure 4.1 and more like Figure 4.2.

Each of us, and each of our students, has schemas like those shown in both of the figures. As we encounter relevant information, we store it in the system we have available. If we have no schema at all, the information will probably "go in one ear and out the other." We have no way of processing the information until a schema for it has been created. Think how many times you may have heard the term "transistor" before you were able to process and retain information about transistors. (Don't feel bad if you still don't have a schema for transistors; many people don't.)

Much of our educational system is devoted to helping students develop their schema systems. That is what a lot of introductory courses are all about. We must get through those introductory courses so we will have the necessary schemas to learn from the more advanced courses. No matter what level we teach, whether it's kindergarten or a graduate seminar, we cannot expect our students to learn the information we convey until we help them develop schemas for that information. If they already have the necessary schema, we need to adapt our communication in such a way that the student can recognize which schema to use. In this way, we can improve students' listening and retention.

Improving Listening and Retention

A case can be made for the assertion that people can be good listeners if they want to be. When we talk to individuals about how to save a lot of money with very little effort, will they listen? You bet. When we talk to them about sex, will they listen?

Most of them will. When we talk to them about long division, will they listen? You can hear them shutting down a mile away.

Yes, listening may be more a product of motivation than one of skill. It may well be, as some argue, that if you show me a person who is not listening, I can show you a poor speaker. This would certainly explain why most listening training programs have only modest success, at best.

Nevertheless, if we want to be effective teachers, we can do quite a bit as sources to help our students be better receivers. Let's look at a few of the things we can do to make our instructional communication more effective.

1. *Be redundant.* Students do not learn everything you want them to know the first time you say it. Sometimes it is necessary to repeat it, as the student may not have heard what you said. Even then, he or she may not understand the message. At this point, it is clear that redundancy is necessary. Repetition is simply the act of restating something exactly as it was said initially. To be redundant is to explain the same thing in more than one way. Some people may understand from just one explanation; others may learn from several different explanations. Conscientious teachers often build in redundancy in their teaching, for they know that any given student does not always learn things the same way another student does. Building in redundancy helps the teacher adapt to students' individual differences without even knowing what those differences are.

2. *Use chunking.* Compare the following:

THEYELLOWCHICKEN	THE YELLOW CHICKEN
233437813	233 43 7813
13042933905	1 304 293 3905

Which column did you find easier to read? If you found the second column easier, you are like most people. The information in both columns is the same, but it is chunked in familiar ways in the second column. The first row is chunked as words, the second as a social security number, and the third as a long-distance telephone number.

Chunking involves breaking information into smaller, more manageable units. In the basketball example we used earlier, we noted that even a professional could not be expected to handle six balls thrown at once. By contrast, even a person with very little athletic skill could catch most of the balls if they were thrown one at a time with a reasonable pause in between. Breaking information down into more manageable units may take a bit longer, but the amount learned will increase so much that it will be well worth the time.

3. *Highlight important information.* Sometimes students do not learn important information because they do not know what is important to know. That is why teachers sometimes get that aggravating question, "Will this be on the test?" This highlighting can be done in many ways. One obvious method is to say things like,

"Be sure to get this, it is important," or, "This will be on the test." Another is to write the important ideas on the chalkboard. Still another is to provide the students with a list of key words or concepts. Of course, the approach that is the most popular in educational circles today is to provide the students with learning objectives for each unit in the course.

It really is remarkable how many students can and will learn what we want them to know if we only care enough to tell them what it is we want them to know. When teachers play "guess what's in my mind" games with students, it may be fun for the teacher, but most of the students concede the game early and take their own minds elsewhere. Students know that not everything in the book will be on the test, but if the instructor does not make clear what parts of the book need to be studied for the test, many students just won't bother to study at all, since they sense that they cannot learn everything. They see the exercise as a game they cannot possibly win, so they decide that studying is a waste of time.

4. *Organize the information.* When possible, teachers need to organize the information according to the students' schema. Sometimes this requires helping the students develop an appropriate schema and then adapting to it. To do this, the teacher needs to have some reasonable organizational pattern for the information that is to be presented. This pattern should not be a secret. The students should be helped to recognize the pattern being followed.

Sometimes teachers indicate their organizational pattern by placing the main points in an outline on the chalkboard or on a projection system. Another method that is effective is to pass out an outline each day. A very effective approach is to have student workbooks that outline what will be discussed in the class and that leave space for students to add their own notes. For example, we found that by providing workbooks for a mass lecture class, we were able to raise the average score on a test from 63 (barely a D) to an average of 84 (a solid B). Lectures and tests were kept the same. Simply adding the outline aided learning that much.

5. *Present information well.* Teachers who present information well will draw attention to that material. While attention is not sufficient to guarantee that learning will occur, lack of attention is sufficient to guarantee that learning will *not* occur. There are many ways of enhancing attention through presentation. These are enumerated in many books related to public communication (e.g., McCroskey, 2006) so they will not be mentioned in detail here. Suffice it to say that teachers who are dynamic and immediate will have a positive impact on their students' attention and learning.

6. *Focus on feedback.* As we will explain in more detail in the next section of this chapter, feedback is a major factor in communication in the classroom. Teachers who attend to nonverbal as well as verbal student feedback are much better able to identify and adapt to those who have trouble understanding or retaining information taught in a class. Ignoring feedback is probably one of the worst things a teacher can do.

Feedback

Except when instructional messages are communicated through a mediated source, and sometimes even then, students are in a position to provide feedback to the teacher. One-way communication has long been known to be anathema to student learning. From the 1950s, when classroom television was trumpeted as the marvelous new teacher, to today's fascination with satellite uplinks and downlinks and the Internet, so-called innovators have come up with ways to replace the live, interactive teacher in the classroom. Mediated systems have proven to be failures because of their inability to accommodate feedback as a real teacher can. Unfortunately, some teachers are also unable to handle feedback. When this is true, one of the primary means of adapting to the needs of students is lost.

Not all feedback is alike, of course. Let us look at the various types.

Positive Feedback

Positive feedback is the type that tells the teacher everything is going well. Positive nods of the head, smiles, and direct eye contact all signal the teacher that the students are with her or him. This is what teachers generally want to see. It is assumed, not always correctly, that if students are giving this kind of feedback, they must be learning.

Negative Feedback

This is pretty much the opposite of positive feedback. It signals to the teacher that something, or many things, are not right. Students looking away, frowning, and shaking their heads are signs that the students are not following or not agreeing with what is being said. Of course, it is possible for feedback to be even more negative, as when students throw things, but this is not the norm in instructional environments. When negative feedback from students is present, it usually is assumed, not always correctly, that learning is not happening.

Absent Feedback

In some instances, students simply sit quietly and provide few responses that could be interpreted as either positive or negative. This absence of clearly interpretable feedback is frequently interpreted by teachers as negative. In fact, this behavior is not necessarily an indication that anything is particularly wrong. Absence of feedback also happens in mediated instruction where no provision for feedback is made. Many teachers cannot handle this type of situation. Some people feel that even negative feedback is better than none.

The impact of the various types of feedback on communication in the instructional setting is highly variable. Figure 4.3 provides a summary that you may find useful. We will go over the information in that figure to make certain it is clear.

Type of Effect	TYPE OF FEEDBACK		
	None	Positive	Negative
Amount of time	Short	Longer	Very long
Accuracy/learning	Low	High	Low or high
Confidence of teacher	Low	High	Low
Confidence of student	Low	High	Low or high
Appropriateness of messages	Low	High	Low or high
Orderliness of class	High	Low	Low

FIGURE 4.3   *Effects of Various Types of Feedback*

Impact of Feedback

We will use the information in the figure to indicate what results the various types of feedback are likely to produce. We will take the categories of effect in the order that they appear in the figure.

Amount of Time to Cover Material

Feedback can have a significant impact on how long it takes to complete an instructional unit. If there is no feedback, the unit simply is presented as planned. There is no need to adapt in any way to the reactions of students if there are no reactions. That is, of course, unless the teacher interprets absent feedback as negative. Whenever that is the case, the effect of no feedback is identical to that of negative feedback. When positive feedback is present, it must be acknowledged, which means presentation of the unit will take a bit longer. Trying to adapt to negative feedback, of course, will take the longest amount of time. Full attention and adaptation to negative feedback may take a very long time indeed.

Accuracy of Learning

An absence of feedback can be associated with a low level of communication accuracy and learning, as any ineffective messages will not be recognized as such. Positive feedback, on the other hand, is associated with high accuracy and learning. The impact of negative feedback depends on the degree to which the teacher adapts to it. If adaptation is minimal, accuracy and learning will be low. If adaptation is high, accuracy and learning may both be greatly enhanced.

Confidence of Teacher

The teacher's confidence that he or she has been effective in communicating with the students is most likely to be low if feedback is negative or if it is missing. By contrast, positive feedback will greatly increase the teacher's confidence.

Confidence of the Student

The students' confidence will parallel that of the teacher under no-feedback and positive feedback conditions. Under negative feedback conditions, confidence will depend on how the teacher adapts to the students' needs. If the adaptation is successful, the confidence of the student will also be high; if the adaptation is unsuccessful, student confidence will also be low.

Appropriateness of Messages

In the absence of feedback, messages are likely to be inappropriate, since there will be no way to know if they should be modified. With positive feedback, of course, messages are very appropriate. With negative feedback, appropriateness is low at least initially. If teacher adaptation is successful, the appropriateness may become high.

Orderliness of the Class

When there is no feedback, the class may be very orderly. Neither positive nor negative feedback is disturbing anyone. However, when feedback is either positive or negative, there is likely to be considerable disturbance. Under positive feedback conditions, that disturbance may be caused by things like laughter or applause, while under negative feedback conditions, it might come from less desirable factors.

It is somewhat difficult to determine which type of feedback is best. Certainly, positive feedback would at least initially be preferred. It does lead to some disorder, however, so students who require high structure and quiet may not find it quite as pleasant as one might expect.

Some teachers might prefer the no-feedback condition. Particularly those who simply want to get the material covered will find this situation most expedient. Those who are most interested in simply carrying messages from one place to another, and who care little about learning, may also find this situation to their liking.

Few teachers are likely to prefer the circumstance where negative feedback is present. At first blush, at least, negative feedback does not appear to be what anyone would want. However, of the three types, negative feedback provides the most needed information. If it does not come when it should, the teacher has no way to know that he or she needs to modify the messages being sent, and learning is less likely to occur. Negative feedback, then, is essential to effective teaching.

Most classrooms provide a mixture of positive and negative feedback. Under the best circumstances, negative feedback produces needed adaptation, which then produces positive feedback. Fortunately, when a concerned teacher is present, such circumstances are far from rare.

References

McCroskey, J. C. (2006). *An introduction to rhetorical communication,* 9th ed. Boston: Allyn & Bacon.
McCroskey, J. C., & Richmond, V. P. (1991). *Quiet children and the classroom teacher,* 2nd ed. Bloomington, IN: ERIC Clearinghouse on Reading and Communication Skills, and Annandale, VA: Speech Communication Association.

Glossary

chunking   Breaking large amounts of information into smaller, more manageable units.
highlighting   Calling attention to particularly important information.
quietness   The tendency of some students and teachers to refrain from talking in the classroom.
redundancy   Repeating the same information in different ways.
rumor   Messages that are exchanged without any proof that the information included is correct.
schemas   Category systems in people's minds that permit the storage of information.
serial communication   A series of communication transactions in which information is passed from person A to person B to person C to person D, and so on.

5

Communication
and Learning Goals

We noted in Chapter 1 that instructional communication is purposeful. In the classroom we have goals and objectives, and the primary function of our communication is the achievement of those goals and objectives. Sometimes our communication does not lead to the achievement of our goals, either because we lose sight of them or because achievement of one goal may interfere with the achievement of another goal. Sometimes goals are not met because teachers really are not aware of the goals they are trying to meet.

Communication Goals

Since it is difficult, if not impossible, for us to control our communication in such a way that it helps us achieve our objectives if we do not really understand those objectives, it is important that we direct some attention to the kinds of goals that teachers typically are trying to attain. These can be categorized as short-term goals and long-term goals.

Short-Term Goals

Short-term goals are the objectives we hope to meet today or within some other limited period of time. Part of the problem with such goals is that, since they seem very limited and obvious, we do not recognize how complex they are and how they may affect other instructional concerns. Let us look at three examples of short-term goals we may have for our students.

1. *To behave in class*. While this is an objective at all levels of instruction, it is particularly important at the elementary school level, since little children are not

born with self-control; it must be taught to them. This may seem like a simple objective—but is it? What do we really mean by "behave"? Does it mean the same thing to the teacher down the hall as it does to you? If not, how does the student distinguish between what you mean and what that other teacher means? Are the same actions "misbehavior" in both classrooms? What does a well-behaved student do? In other words, how do you know one when you see one? Can you tell when your goal is met?

2. *To study the lesson.* This is a short-term goal professed by teachers at all levels of instruction. But, again, what does it mean? Do we mean study in class, or at home, or both? How will you know whether the student does or does not study? Do you really care, or are you just mouthing what you were taught teachers are supposed to say? Would you be willing to settle for having the student just behave in class?

3. *To accomplish course objectives.* This is the real bottom line for most teachers. But do you have expressed objectives? Do the students know what they are? If not, why not? Are you playing the old game of "Guess what's in my mind"? Do you enjoy catching students who haven't studied by asking tricky questions? Are you certain you really know what the students need to learn?

While these examples do not represent all of the short-term objectives teachers have, they should give you a sense of the potential for problems in the classroom. If the teacher does not clearly understand her or his goals, how can the student be expected to understand them? If the teacher understands the goals but does not communicate them to the student, how can the student be expected to understand them? What is the priority order of the goals? Is behaving in class more important than accomplishing course learning objectives? Is it more important that the student learn to diagram sentences or that he or she learn to enjoy studying the language?

Long-Term Goals

Long-term goals are those that are aimed at what will become of the student later on, well after he or she no longer is in our class. These goals may deal with such global concerns as the student becoming a good citizen and a contributing member of society. They may focus on helping her or him develop an appreciation for art, music, or literature; adopt a healthy lifestyle; or become a lifelong learner. They also may be concerned with somewhat more immediate issues, such as choosing to enroll in another course in the subject matter you teach, being able to perform satisfactorily in an advanced course that follows yours, or choosing a career that draws from the subject you teach.

To acknowledge a common analogy, the long-term goals are the forest while the short-term goals are the trees. Often we lose sight of the long-term goals, which are much more central to what education is all about, and focus virtually all of our communication efforts on the immediate concerns related to short-term goals. If teachers focus only on short-term goals, students will naturally learn to do likewise. They may come to believe that all learning is temporary and that forgetting what they learned last semester is not only acceptable but normal, possibly even necessary.

For a teacher to focus on short-term goals may be, at least in part, a function of that teacher being sensitive to her or his limitations. As educators we often see ourselves as having a very limited span of control. That is, we feel we can have a direct impact only on those students who are in our classes right now. It is certainly easier to see the effect we have on those students, but that does not mean our influence stops when the student completes our class. In fact, most of our important influences (positive or negative) will come later. If we turn a student on to what we teach, that student will likely succeed in later courses in that subject matter. If we turn that student off to the subject, he or she may not succeed in the course, much less take another course in the area, much less succeed in the course in the area.

It is important that teachers not only recognize their potential for having long-term impact but that they also consciously enhance the possibilities of the positive impact they may have. Sometimes long-term goals are sacrificed in the interest of meeting short-term objectives. Teachers need to determine what goals are most important, and never lose sight of those goals.

Learning Objectives: A Communication Perspective

The field of educational psychology has long acknowledged the benefit of establishing learning objectives for instruction (Bloom, 1956; Krathwohl, Bloom, & Masia, 1964). Consequently, almost all teachers have studied the nature and use of learning objectives. We will briefly describe the major domains of learning objectives here, not to be redundant with your previous exposure but as an introduction to a communication perspective on these objectives, since they have been seen as central to the study of communication in instruction since the earliest writings in this area (Hurt, Scott, & McCroskey, 1978).

There are three broad domains of learning objectives: cognitive, psychomotor, and affective. We will consider each in turn.

Cognitive Domain

The cognitive domain of learning has to do with the process of acquiring knowledge. At the lowest level, knowledge refers to a specific unit of information, such as the date of a historical event, how to define a given word, or what a driver is expected to do when he or she sees a stop sign. At the middle level, knowledge relates to methods of inquiry, such as hypothesis testing, generalizations or principles, and larger theories. At the highest level, knowledge is concerned with the ability to interpret, analyze, and synthesize the knowledge acquired at the lower levels and the new information with which the learner will come into contact later.

Learning objectives in the cognitive domain tend to center on the lower knowledge level in early childhood education and in beginning courses in high school and college, and move to the higher knowledge levels as the student progressively moves to more advanced instruction in a subject area. Thus, even in many college courses, since students have not been introduced to the subject matter previously, learning objectives may center on the lowest level of the cognitive domain. A primary function of such courses is to establish schemas for processing information in the particular subject area. If the student does not continue taking courses in that area, then the student may not be able deal with complex theories, much less develop the cognitive skills necessary to interpret, analyze, and synthesize information in that subject.

Psychomotor Domain

While the cognitive domain is concerned with the "knowing," the psychomotor domain is concerned with the "doing." At the lowest level, this domain relates to basic control of physical behaviors, such as a baby learning to hold a rattle handed to her or him by a parent or focusing her or his eyes on a toy hanging over the bed. At the middle level, psychomotor learning relates to such behaviors as writing, walking, running, jumping, and throwing. At the highest levels, this domain centers on more complex behaviors such as typing, speaking a foreign language, playing a piano or some other musical instrument, driving a vehicle or replacing the engine in a vehicle, or shooting a basketball while five other people are trying to take it away.

Learning objectives in this area tend to be highly valued in the lower grades, but they seem to lose their importance in educational systems at higher levels. Consider the relative importance ascribed to English and mathematics, for example, compared with driver education and typing, even though the latter two may save a person's life or permit her or him to work with the most sophisticated computers!

Affective Domain

The affective domain of learning is concerned with the student's attitudes, beliefs, and values as they relate to the cognitive and psychomotor skills he or she has acquired. The affective domain is associated with a student's behavioral choices. A person may know what to do and have the psychomotor skills to do it, but if he or she does not have a positive attitude toward the behavior, it probably will not get done. This domain of learning is the one that receives the least attention from many teachers. In fact, many teachers openly decry any focus on the affective domain at all. Almost all of us have heard at least one teacher say something like, "I was hired to teach kids math. It is not my job to make them like it!"

Well, maybe it isn't. Achievement tests given in many areas of the country include measures of affect for the subject matter. Average scores on both the cognitive achievement tests and the affective evaluations are reported to the school system, but only the cognitive results are regularly published in the newspapers. A notable exception to that pattern was a report that appeared in the national newspaper *USA Today* in 1998. The newspaper conveyed the same information that was covered on the network newscasts, which indicated that students in the United States scored near the bottom on math and science tests compared with selected students in several other countries. Unlike most other national news sources, they also noted that the students in the United States had scored higher than the students from all of the other countries in their attitudes toward math. But this information was dismissed as unimportant, since it had not produced higher cognitive learning scores. The fact that positive attitudes toward subject matter are likely to be the precursors of subsequent learning was never mentioned, nor was the fact that positive attitudes had not been the norm for earlier testing of the same type. Thus, what could have been seen as some of the best news with regard to the teaching of mathematics in the United States in many years was reported as another failure in that field. It should be noted that this newspaper is not singled out here to be criticized, for at least it reported the attitude results. Most other newspapers and television newsrooms considered these results so unnewsworthy that they did not even acknowledge such information was available. Many teachers do not even know that this data is available, because administrators who receive the reports do not consider them of any consequence. This is most unfortunate.

If the school system and the public that pays for that system do not care about affective learning, maybe they do not believe that the teacher is responsible for generating it. But if not, then who is responsible for such learning?

If teachers are responsible for teaching students a cognitive understanding of good government, who is responsible for generating the positive affect for that subject? If teachers are responsible for teaching students a cognitive understanding of the harm that nicotine, alcohol, and other drugs can do to the body, who is responsible for generating the negative affect toward such substances? If the fifth-grade teacher is responsible for generating a cognitive understanding of how to diagram sentences, who is responsible for generating the positive affect for understanding the language and using it well? If the third-grade teacher is responsible for ensuring that students attain cognitive mastery of the times tables, who is responsible for generating the positive affect for learning math and science?

Almost all of our long-term goals for education are based on appropriate affective learning. Thus, if we focus all of our attention on short-term cognitive and psychomotor objectives, is it any wonder that our long-term objectives often are not met?

Communication and Learning in Perspective

As just stated, from a communication perspective at least, the affective domain of learning is critical. But this certainly is not the view most commonly expressed in education circles or in public hearings about how to improve education. Nor is this lack of attention to the affective domain a recent development. Throughout history, attention has been focused primarily on cognitive learning and, to a lesser extent, on psychomotor learning. Attention to affective learning has frequently been missing entirely.

From antiquity, education has involved a live teacher and student communicating. Such interaction has been at the heart of virtually all instructional systems throughout recorded history.

Innovations, however, have often been sought to replace or at least supplement the teacher with another medium. The printing of books was seen as a marvelous extension of the teacher-cum-author, one that would permit teaching many, many more students at very low cost. Later, the development of the radio provided another marvelous extension of the teacher-cum-radio personality, one that would permit taking the teacher's voice to the far corners of the remote regions of the world. In succession, we have evolved from radio to television (remember those "talking heads"?) to computers to satellites that can carry both television and computer signals to the farthest corners of the world, and now to the Internet. The communications revolutions have occurred. So education has been greatly improved, right?

Not quite. Remember the difference between *communications* and *communication* that we noted in Chapter 1? All of these innovations have involved simply getting messages to people more expediently (communications). None have dealt with what was contained in the messages (communication).

Some innovations, however, have focused on the quality of the messages themselves. Programmed instruction delivered through either books or computers has proven to be quite successful in teaching low-level cognitive objectives. In fact, some research suggests that this method is superior to instruction from a live teacher, for the computer is more tolerant of error and better able to repeat itself over and over in a wide variety of ways without exhaustion than any live teacher could be expected to be. Before you panic about how you are going to be replaced by the computer, consider what we know about computers so far. We know that computers, at least to this point, are not able to successfully produce desired affective learning either as well or as cheaply as live teachers. However, there is no denying that this is something they may be able to do in the future, as anyone who has seen a child mesmerized by a computer game is most likely to attest. That is, computers, if appropriately programmed by teachers-cum-programmers, may be able to produce affective learning as successfully as a live teacher. Given what the society is willing to pay live teachers, it is doubtful the criterion of "cheapness" will ever be overcome!

The big problem with most of the improvements in communications is that they get old for the learner quite quickly. At first, they really do work, and the student likes them, and that liking can rub off on the content being taught. But then the novelty wears off, and the innovation loses its impact. The student wants to return to the "old" method, with a "real teacher." People, including students, need to communicate with other people. Thus communication, not communications, is the teacher's most important tool. And that tool is most important as it relates to the affective domain of learning.

It is important that we do not give the impression that cognitive and psychomotor learning are unimportant. Far from that, they are vitally important. But they are not enough to come close to meeting the long-term objectives of educational systems. If they receive all of the attention, and affective learning is ignored or given only an occasional nod, the system cannot meet its most important goals.

When we communicate with students, we provide them with content related to the cognitive and/or psychomotor domains. But, even more important, we also communicate with them in such a way that we express our own affect for the content we teach. Thus, we are going to communicate affectively with our students; it is only a question of what kind of affect we communicate. If we make learning our subject matter an unpleasant task with no apparent intrinsic rewards, the affect we will generate will be negative. If we communicate the subject's value, the outcome will be more positive. The remainder of this book focuses primarily on just that.

References

Bloom, B. S., ed. (1956). *Taxonomy of educational objectives: Handbook I. Cognitive domain.* New York: McKay.

Hurt, H. T., Scott, M. D., & McCroskey, J. C. (1978). *Communication in the classroom.* Reading, MA: Addison-Wesley.

Krathwohl, D. R., Bloom, B. S., & Masia, B. B. (1964). *Taxonomy of educational objectives: Handbook II. Affective domain.* New York: McKay.

Glossary

affective learning   The process of developing attitudes, beliefs, and values associated with areas of cognitive and psychomotor learning.

cognitive learning   The process of acquiring, integrating, and synthesizing knowledge.

psychomotor learning   The process of mastering psychomotor behaviors.

6

Selectivity and Communication

Students learn what they choose to learn, not what we choose for them to learn. That means we need to figure out how to get them to choose to learn the same things we choose to teach them. That is the critical challenge all teachers must face.

Getting through to students is not an easy task under the best of circumstances. Even if we have a highly motivated student who really wants to learn what we want to teach, the odds are still against success unless we can win the "selectivity battles" we face. The noise in the receiver, which we noted in our model of the instructional communication process (Figure 1.1), is not there because the student wants it there; it is there because the student is a human being (McCroskey & Wheeless, 1976).

Human beings are information processors. That is, messages do not simply go directly from their source to the mind of the receiver; they go through a reception and processing system. Most messages do not get through that system at all. Those that do may be modified greatly before the meaning they are meant to generate is stored in the receiver's mind. That meaning may be only remotely related to the meaning the source was attempting to communicate.

In a very real sense, trying to get our messages to produce student learning is like trying to make our way through an obstacle course. The obstacles are the various types of selectivity, as illustrated in Figure 6.1. We must overcome each obstacle in turn, for at any point our message may be blocked from stimulating the meaning we want to communicate. If we fail to recognize an obstacle, or to deal with that obstacle, our instructional goals will be missed.

As indicated in Figure 6.1, there are four types of selectivity that can directly interfere with initial learning: selective exposure, selective attention, selective perception, and selective retention. A fifth type of selectivity may occur even after initial learning has occurred: selective recall. We will look at each of these in turn.

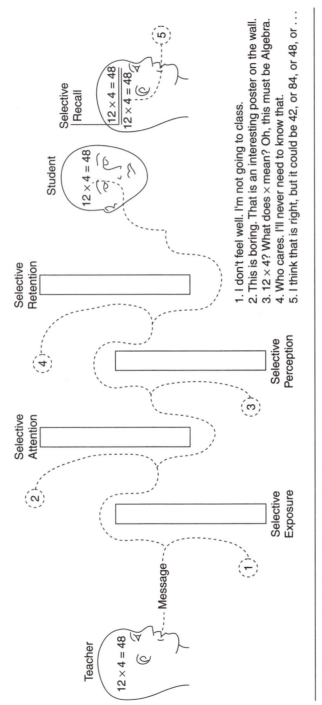

FIGURE 6.1 *Selectivity and Information Processing*

1. I don't feel well. I'm not going to class.
2. This is boring. That is an interesting poster on the wall.
3. 12 × 4? What does × mean? Oh, this must be Algebra.
4. Who cares. I'll never need to know that.
5. I think that is right, but it could be 42, or 48, or . . .

Selective Exposure

Selective exposure refers to a person's conscious or unconscious decision to place her- or himself in a position to receive messages from a particular source. We all engage in this type of behavior every day. When we choose a television channel, we have selectively exposed ourselves. Even if we just turn on the TV and watch whatever is on the channel to which it was turned by someone else, we have selectively exposed ourselves, for we chose not to change the channel.

Students sometimes have the option of choosing what course they want to take. If we teach an elective course, we can reasonably assume that the students in the class will be more motivated to learn in that class than students in required courses would be. And, by the way, why is it that we have required courses such as English, foreign languages, or math? Is it because we think such classes would be good for the students? Not really. That would be a good reason for offering the classes, but in fact the reason we require them is that we don't think the students would selectively expose themselves to those courses otherwise!

Students sometimes have a choice of different teachers for the same course, particularly at the college level. In such cases, the student can choose to selectively expose her- or himself to one teacher and not to others. This makes some teachers uncomfortable or even jealous of other teachers. Teachers who are regularly selected are often described in negative ways by their less-frequently-selected colleagues. Since one teacher is more popular than another, the popular teacher must be doing something dreadful, or so the rumors typically go.

If we are going to control students' selective exposure behaviors and use them to our advantage in enhancing the students' learning, we need to understand what factors lead to exposure decisions. Let us consider several.

Proximity

That which is immediately available is most likely to be chosen. Universities have learned that classes offered in student dormitories are very popular. Even if it is not precisely what the student wants, its proximity makes it likely to be chosen. A large proportion of young people attend colleges within a few miles of their homes. While cost is an important consideration, another important factor is that the school is close to home and easy to get to. If a student needs an answer to a question, a peer sitting close by is closer than the teacher and is more likely to be asked the question.

Involvement

The more important a topic is to a person, the more the person is likely to expose her- or himself to messages on that topic. Sixteen-year-old students are likely to be very involved in getting their driving licenses. Hence, they are likely to selectively expose themselves to a driver education course or to reading a booklet on the information one needs to pass the license examination. Although a basketball player may have low involvement with English, he or she is likely to be highly involved with basketball practice. Attendance at English class is not as probable as attendance at basketball practice, and if there is a conflict between the two, we can be virtually certain of which one will be selected for exposure.

Utility

Things that are seen as immediately useful are more likely to be selected for exposure than those that have little immediate utility. If a student has a test in math tomorrow and one in history next week, if he or she is going to study tonight, odds are that it will be on math, not on history. This applies to various other types of subject matter as well. That which the student sees as useful in life now, rather than in some distant future time, will draw much more exposure.

Reinforcement

People expose themselves to messages they believe will be consistent with their own beliefs. Democrats go to Democratic party rallies. Republicans go to Republican party rallies. When we attend athletic events, we sit on "our" side of the field, not "their" side. Pro-choice people listen to and read messages that support a woman's right to an abortion. Pro-life people listen to and read messages that advocate the abolition of abortion. In short, we all want to hear others present messages that agree with our own views, and we only infrequently choose to expose ourselves to messages that we know in advance will take positions with which we disagree. Students will seek the advice of teachers they consider "with it" but will avoid hearing advice from those they see as out of date or out of touch with people their age.

Whatever the reason students engage in selective exposure, the bottom line remains the same: No exposure, no learning. Getting the student to be present and hear and see the message does not guarantee that he or she will learn from that message, but failing to get the student to be present does guarantee the student will not learn from it. Exposure is a necessary but not sufficient condition for learning.

Selective Attention

As the old saying goes, you can bring a horse to water (selective exposure), but you can't make it drink (selective attention). Students cannot always control the type of messages they are exposed to from teachers. Hence, when they are exposed to messages they would rather avoid, they may simply select to pay attention to something else. In a sense, all attention is selective. Everything in our students' perceptual world makes some demand upon their attention, but they cannot attend to everything at once. They may choose to attend to something other than our messages, or they may pay more attention to some of our messages and less to others.

A myriad of things in the normal classroom call out to students for their attention: other students, things going on outside the windows, things on the walls or posted on bulletin boards, the teacher's clothing, something on a nearby desk, the clock, and on and on. Many factors, then, determine what the student will pay attention to. Let us consider a few of those.

Attention Span

No matter what a student chooses to attend to, that attention can continue only so long. The time a person can spend attending to one thing is referred to as her or his attention span. How long that span will be depends in part on developmental factors. Young children typically have very brief attention spans, while adult attention spans are longer. No one, however, has an attention span that extends as long as even the shortest of class periods. Attention spans are typically measured in seconds, not minutes. Students' attention, of necessity, will move from one thing to another during a class period. Any teacher who expects full and undivided attention for an entire class period is expecting the impossible. That is one reason that redundancy, which we discussed in Chapter 4, is so important. When we teach things redundantly, students may miss the point once while attending to something else but attend to it and learn another time.

Novelty

Things that are unusual attract attention. When someone who is not a regular member of the class (like the principal) enters the room, virtually everyone's attention is directed toward that person. Similarly, things that can be seen out a window often command attention because they are novel. The senior author recalls his attention once being drawn away from what he was teaching by a tree going past the windows of his classroom. While that would have been unusual in any circumstance, in this case, he was teaching on the fifth floor! Needless to say, the students' attention was also riveted on the tree. Everyone went to the windows to see the groundskeepers with a huge truck and crane slowly moving a tree that was at least 80 feet tall down the street to be planted in front of a new library building.

This example indicates that there are times when the teacher has no realistic hope of recapturing students' attention from truly novel events. To persist in teaching only guarantees failure. Fortunately, such extremely novel events happen rarely. However, events that are just "a little bit novel" are often enough to redirect attention. This presents the teacher with both a challenge and an opportunity. While uncontrolled novelty can pull student attention away from the teacher, intentionally introducing novelty can capture attention for the teacher. If the novelty is associated with the material being taught, it will facilitate learning.

Concreteness

Highly abstract material bores students, so they search their surroundings for other places to direct their attention. Concrete things or ideas, on the other hand, attract attention. Nothing will help students understand such abstract concepts as freedom of speech or freedom of the press, and realize why people are willing to risk their lives to defend them, more than having the principal or school board impose censorship on the school newspaper by restricting what the students can include in it. Students who may have been so bored they were sleeping in political science class last week may be marching in front of the school this week. This is the difference between the abstract and the concrete in terms of their ability to capture attention.

Fortunately, we do not have to create such emotion-charged issues as censorship of the paper to bring concreteness into the classroom. The key is to relate whatever you are teaching to the real-life experience of the learner whenever possible. This is not always easy, but most things worth teaching have some relationship to the concrete world, if the teacher will only look hard enough to find it.

Size

As a rule, bigger things draw more attention than smaller ones. When designing visual aids for instruction, then, bigger is better under most circumstances. Big maps, big pictures, and big graphs will grab attention.

Duration

Attention is directed to things that are moderate in duration. Lessons that are very short may be over before some of the students tune in. Similarly, those that go on for a long time may exceed the student's capacity to stay with them. However, judicious use of breaks to allow students to attend to other matters may permit sufficient attention to be given to matters that take longer to teach.

Whatever the reason for the students' use of selective attention, as we said with selective exposure, the bottom line is the same: No attention, no learning. Although attention is not sufficient to guarantee learning, the absence of attention will guarantee that learning will not occur. Attention is a necessary but not sufficient condition for learning.

Selective Perception

Perception is the process of ascribing meaning to messages. As we noted in Chapter 2, messages do not "carry" meaning. They stimulate meaning. What meaning is stimulated is a function of both the message and the receiver. Thus, in a sense, all perception is selective. The receiver must select, from all the possible meanings that could be ascribed to a message, the particular meaning that should be ascribed in the given instance. Hence, it is most likely that different receivers of the same message will ascribe different meanings to it. The challenge for the teacher is to get the student to ascribe the meaning of the teacher's choice rather than some other meaning. This is more likely to happen when we can control factors that may lead to other perceptions, although it usually is not possible to control all of the possibilities.

Even if we get the student to expose her- or himself to our messages and to pay attention to those messages, the desired learning may not occur because the student may perceive the messages to mean something different than what was intended. A number of factors influence such perceptions or, at least from the teacher's perspective, misperceptions. Let us examine several of these factors.

Ambiguity of Messages

Sometimes messages are very imprecise and open to misunderstanding. Use of words that can be interpreted in different ways can lead a student to select a meaning other than the one intended. Since language is inherently imprecise, careful choice of wording is very important if one hopes to avoid being misunderstood. Use of abstract rather than concrete words and phrases is particularly problematic. In general, the more concrete and specific a message is, the less likely it is to be misperceived; the more abstract a series of messages is, the more likely those messages are to be misperceived.

Lack of Redundancy

When a series of messages lacks redundancy, those messages invite misperceptions. Redundancy permits a second (or third, fourth, and so on) chance for the student to select the teacher's intended meaning. Single messages are far more likely to be misunderstood than multiple messages directed toward stimulating the same meaning.

Lack of Schema

As we noted in Chapter 4, if students do not have appropriate schemas for the ideas that teachers introduce, they may not be able to cope with those ideas. When we hear an idea expressed, we search our schema systems for where the idea belongs. If we find no place at all, the idea will probably just pass on through the system and not really be perceived at all. If, however, we find a place that seems to be appropriate, even though it is not, we will select to perceive that idea as if it did belong there. Thus, we will have a perception that may be quite different from that which the person expressing the idea had intended. Thus, the child may perceive an "invisible nation" rather than an "indivisible nation" in the pledge of allegiance because the adult did not realize that the child was too young to comprehend what the words in the pledge were intended to convey. Once again, if we are to expect students to understand what we teach, we must be certain they have the necessary schema in place before we teach—or we must teach the schema.

Previous Experiences

We know the world through our experiences with the world. The experiences of a child in the 1960s are not the same as the experiences of a child in the early twenty-first century. It is vital that teachers draw on the experiences of the learner, as opposed to their own experiences, whenever possible. There is almost always a generation gap between teachers and students, the exceptions most often being at the college level. The longer a teacher continues in the profession, the larger that gap becomes. Thus, each year it becomes both more important to strive to adapt to the experiences of one's students and at the same time more difficult to do so.

Another aspect of experience relates to exposure to the subject matter itself. It is not uncommon, except at the lowest levels of education, for students to have previously been taught some of the content in any given field. If that experience was positive, the present experience is more likely to be viewed positively. If it was negative, the present learning experience may be judged that way also. In addition, the student may have learned something incorrectly before, either because of her or his misperceptions or because it was taught incorrectly. That information may get in the way of new information and may lead to selective perceptions that are not what the teacher intends. Encouraging student interaction in the instructional process is a good way to draw out such misperceptions so they can be corrected before the student files them away for future reference.

Expectancies and Biases

We will consider expectancies in more detail in Chapter 9. An expectancy is an anticipation of a future occurrence. A bias is an unjustified evaluation. All people, including students, have both expectancies and biases. They have expectancies for how teachers will behave and what they will say. And they have biases toward the subject matter being taught (for example, "I hate English, particularly poems!"). Even if the teacher does not behave in the expected way or say the expected things, it is likely that these expectancies and biases will influence how the teacher's messages will be perceived. This is particularly true when the teacher and the student have little or no history of interaction. As the student gets to know the teacher better, the student's expectancies may be modified to be more in line with this particular teacher's normal behaviors. Similarly, initial biases may be put aside and replaced by an attitude toward the subject matter that reflects the way it is being taught in the specific class. As a result, it is a wise teacher who takes some time early in a course to work on developing positive relationships with the students so that this excess baggage of expectancies and biases will have less impact on the students' perceptions of the teacher's messages.

Selective perception is a difficult problem for a teacher to overcome, because it will always occur to some extent. If a student does not accurately perceive the content that is being taught, the intended cognitive or psychomotor learning cannot occur. Even after overcoming selective exposure and selective attention, instruction can fail because of misperceptions of content. One positive thing is that even if misperceptions occur, if they can be identified, they can still be corrected. Regular testing is the best way to determine that inappropriate perceptions have resulted in faulty cognitive or psychomotor learning. When such problems are identified, remedial instruction can be introduced to resolve those problems. If they are not identified, however, the mislearning will stay with the learner, and the instructional outcome may actually be worse than if no instruction had been attempted at all.

Selective Retention

Selective retention may well be the problem that frustrates teachers the most. Students are present, they pay attention, and, through interaction with them, we know they perceived what they were being taught. But a few days (or sometimes minutes!) later, they seem never to have heard of the ideas before. Selective retention refers to the decision to store or not store information in long-term memory. As with the other selectivity factors, this process occurs primarily at the unconscious level, but the selection is sometimes made consciously. Several factors are known to influence selective retention.

Lack of Highlighting

When important ideas are not highlighted by teachers, students often do not realize they are important. This is one of the reasons why providing students with learning objectives is such a good idea. Although this is only one of the many means of highlighting, it represents a very clear message to the student about what the teacher expects her or him to retain. When information seems to go in one ear and out the other, highlighting through objectives can serve as an effective earplug.

Lack of Redundancy

In general, the more we hear something, the more important we think it is. Redundancy capitalizes on this premise. Sometimes people simply do not think something is important until they hear it several times. For children, this concept is particularly important. In contrast to adults, children are exposed to vastly more new things each day. They cannot be expected to retain everything new they learn initially. If we expect a child to learn something, we need to teach it more than once, and in more than one way.

Lack of Schema

Schemas are very important to initial learning, and they are absolutely critical for retention. If there is no system for storage (schema) available, there will be no storage. It is like trying to store information on a computer with no hard drive. You turn it off, and the information is gone. The student's schema is the hard drive. If it is missing or defective, retention will not occur. The reason so much of our education is devoted to teaching students the same things they have been taught previously is that material is often not taught with retention in mind. Rather than simply assuming students will retain what they initially learn, it is critical that they be taught *how* to retain the information. It does not come naturally!

Lack of Realistic Application

Retention often depends on applying new information to real, present situations. Learning for some indefinite future use is particularly difficult. If we incorporate present experience into the teaching of new information, it is more likely to be retained. As the saying goes, children who see and hear, understand; children who do, remember.

Primacy and Recency Laws

Several decades ago, social scientists who were very interested in persuasion sought to determine whether things that were covered first (the primacy principle) or things that were covered last (the recency principle) were most remembered (Hovland, Janis, & Kelley, 1953). After many studies, it became clear that neither primacy nor recency had a universally stronger effect than the other. However, there was evidence that things presented either near the beginning or near the end of the message would be more readily perceived than things presented in the middle. The advice to teachers, then, is that what you want students to retain should be stressed at the beginning of the unit or at the end of the unit—or, better yet, at both the beginning and the ending.

        The bottom line is that if you do not teach for retention, you are not likely to get retention. In Chapter 2, we noted that telling is not communicating. Telling is not teaching, either. Simply presenting information, no matter how clearly, will not ensure retention. Only teaching for retention can raise that probability.

Selective Recall

Selective retention and selective recall are often confused and sometimes thought to be the same thing. It is important to distinguish between these two forms of selectivity because they are quite different, though related. Selective retention has to with the storage of information, while selective recall has to do with the retrieval of information. Of course, if information is not stored (retained) in the first place, it cannot be retrieved (recalled) later. However, the mere fact that something is retained does not necessarily mean it will be recalled at any given point in time. Have you ever had a hard time recalling something at one time but had it come back to you at another time? It was stored away in your brain at both times, but it was only retrieved once.

        If a teacher wants to know whether instruction has been retained, he or she must be certain to test for recall of information in the way that the information was taught. Otherwise, the learner may have indeed retained the information but may not be stimulated to recall it because the testing procedure does not trigger recall from the place where the information is stored. When students say things like, "Oh, that is what you wanted to know. I didn't understand the question," they may just be giving a lame excuse. More likely, however, what the student is expressing is that he or she was attempting to recall the information but couldn't find it because he or she was looking in the wrong place. You can't find what you stored in the garage if you are looking for it in all of the closets.

Sometimes we teach things that we expect students to generalize to another, new context. While this sort of generalization may occur by chance occasionally, one should not expect it on a regular basis. Such "transfer of training" has been the object of much research during the past century. It has been argued, for example, that if people study Latin, they will understand English better, or that if we teach people to give speeches without experiencing stage fright, they will overcome their general shyness. The research in this area suggests that expecting such transfer of training, or generalization of learning, is frequently no more than wishful thinking.

Transfer is likely to occur when what is learned in one context has virtually the same application in another context, and the learner recognizes that application (Bugelski, 1964). If a child learns to stand for the playing of the U.S. national anthem, we can expect the child to stand for the Canadian anthem only if the child knows two things: (1) a person should stand for all national anthems, and (2) what I am hearing here in Toronto is the Canadian national anthem. Learners need to be taught to generalize appropriately, or transfer should not be expected. If we only teach the student to stand for one anthem, we should not expect her or him to figure out that is a rule for all anthems. Thus, if we ask a question like, "What should you do when you hear the song 'O Canada' in Canada?" we should not be surprised if the student responds with either, "Listen," or, "I don't know." We cannot expect any student to recall what was never taught. Even when it is taught, learned, and retained, it can still sometimes be difficult to recall.

Students only learn what they select to learn, and they only retain what they select to retain. Thus, for students to learn and retain information over time, teachers must gear their communication toward producing such effects. Students respond to the need for selectivity because that is the normal human response, not because they do not want to learn. It should be expected that the student will not know about the selectivity processes. It is up to the teacher to understand these processes and to prepare students to overcome them in the learning environment. If the teacher does not do this, who will?

References

Bugelski, B. R. (1964). *The psychology of learning applied to teaching*. Indianapolis, IN: Bobbs-Merrill.

Hovland, C. I., Janis, I. L., & Kelley, H. H. (1953). *Communication and persuasion*. New Haven, CT: Yale University Press.

McCroskey, J. C., & Wheeless, L. R. (1976). *An introduction to human communication*. Boston: Allyn & Bacon.

Glossary

attention span   The period of time during which an individual receives messages from a given source.

expectancy   Anticipation of a future occurrence.

involvement   The relative importance a topic is seen to have by an individual.

selective attention   The degree to which a set of messages are selected to be received by an individual.

selective exposure   A person's decision to place him- or herself in a position to receive messages from a particular source.

selective perception   The process of a receiver interpreting messages received from a source.

selective recall   The retrieval of information from storage.

selective retention   The decision to store or not store information in long-term memory.

transfer of training   An alleged generalization of learning in one context to another context.

utility   The degree to which a person perceives something to be immediately useful.

7

Teacher Images

No message is interpreted by a receiver apart from its source. In fact, the source–message relationship is so strong that it has been found that receivers will create a source in their minds if the real source is unknown (McCroskey & Dunham, 1966). There appears to be an inherent realization in people that to understand and evaluate a message, we need to know who the source of the message was. Nearly 2,500 years ago, the great philosophers and rhetoricians of the day were well aware that the image or ethos of a speaker had a major influence on the impact of the speaker's message. Aristotle, Cicero, Plato, and Quintillion all stressed this source–message relationship in their speaking and writing.

People will grasp at almost anything to create the needed image of the unknown source. It has been found, for example, that when an unknown source is introduced by someone we know, we transfer much of the introducer's image to that unknown person. This has been called the sponsorship effect (Holtzman, 1966; McCroskey & Dunham, 1966). One place where use of the sponsorship effect is most obvious is in political campaigns, where unknown candidates make sure to have prominent local people introduce them to the audience.

Contemporary social psychologists explain the role of the message source in how a receiver responds to a message in terms of several theories that collectively have generated what has come to be known as the principle of consistency (Brown, 1965). The essence of this principle is that if two attitudes (or perceptions, beliefs, or values) are inconsistent with each other, change in one or both occurs because of the mind's efforts to establish and maintain consistency. This need for consistency occurs in all people. While we can tolerate some inconsistency, the greater it becomes, the more pressure we feel to resolve it.

Another thing that people of all cultures and backgrounds share is that they all have certain common beliefs. Examples include notions like these: "Good people agree with me." "Bad people disagree with me." "Good people tell the truth." "Bad people lie." When we hear someone we like say something we dislike, we are pressured to change our minds about the person, what he or she has said, or both. The stronger our liking and respect for the person, the more difficult it is for us to disregard what he or she says as false or irrelevant.

Effects of Teacher Images

Teacher images, like those of other message sources, are critical to the impact of teacher communication on students. Much of that impact can best be understood by referring to our discussion in Chapter 6 of the selectivity process.

Selective Exposure

Students who have a positive image of the teacher are more likely to expose themselves to communication from that teacher. That is, they are more likely to sign up for a class the teacher offers, they are more likely to attend that class and sit in a place where it is easy to see and hear the teacher, and they are more likely to seek communication with the teacher outside the class. Students who have a negative image of the teacher will try to avoid her or him when possible. They will refuse to sign up for a class with that teacher unless forced to do so, avoid prominent seating positions, cut class, and limit contact with the teacher outside of class. In short, a teacher's image is a central factor in students' selective exposure to that teacher.

Selective Attention

Students who have a positive image of the teacher are initially more likely to pay attention to what the teacher is saying. They are also more likely to return attention to the teacher after momentary distractions. Students who have a negative image of the teacher are likely to attend to other stimuli while the teacher is talking, or simply to daydream. As with exposure, the teacher's image is central to students' selective attention to that teacher.

Selective Perception

Students who have a positive image of the teacher are more likely to perceive what he or she says the way the teacher intended it to be perceived. Such perceptions tend to be generalized to positive attitudes toward the subject matter being taught. That is, the general belief that "good people teach good subjects" is confirmed.

On the other hand, Murphy's law, which says that anything that can go wrong will go wrong, tends to apply when the teacher has a negative image. So not only is it more likely that students will misperceive what the teacher says, but it is also more likely that the message will be perceived in a negative way. These negative reactions are likely to carry over to the subject matter the teacher is conveying. This is consistent with the general belief that "bad people teach bad subjects."

Selective Retention

Students want to learn from a teacher for whom they hold a positive image. They consider the information he or she teaches to be positive and valuable. Thus, they are likely to try harder to retain information they receive from a teacher with a positive image. Students have little motivation to learn from teachers for whom they hold a negative image. They consider information such teachers present to be of little value and therefore make only a minimal effort to retain what they do learn. In fact, while they may study the content for a test, they may actively try to put the information out of their minds after that test.

Selective Recall

Recalling information is a tricky process at best. One of the things that mentally healthy people do is push unpleasant experiences far back into their memories where they will not be referenced regularly. By contrast, pleasant memories are often replayed and enjoyed over and over. Since learning from a teacher whose image is positive is generally a pleasant experience, memories of the experience are more likely to be recalled by the student. About the only exception to that rule is when students or former students are sharing stories about unpleasant experiences in school. Then the teacher with the worst image is likely to be recalled.

Clearly, the image students have of a teacher is highly related to those students' learning. That image cannot be ignored if the teacher is to maximize the learning of her or his students. A teacher who does not care about her or his image may be interested in talking but definitely is not interested in teaching.

Because a teacher's image is so closely related to her or his effectiveness, the nature and components of that image need to be understood and managed. It is useful for us to think of the teacher's image as the sum total of all of the perceptions of the teacher in the student's mind. Although there is no limit to the number of perceptions that can exist, there are certain categories of perceptions that research suggests are particularly important. We will direct our attention to those categories for the remainder of this chapter.

Before we turn to these matters, however, we need to stress that the image of the teacher exists in only one place: the mind of the student. It is, in essence, the meaning the student has for the teacher; thus, it can exist only in the student's mind. A teacher's image, therefore, is not portable. He or she cannot take it from one class to another or from one job to another. While a teacher's reputation can have some effect on a student's image of the teacher before the two have ever met, what the teacher says and does in the classroom will, in the vast majority of cases, have the most impact on the image the student will have. It should come as no surprise, then, that a given teacher may have a very different image in one class than in another. To the extent that a teacher says and does things differently in the two classes, that is to be expected.

Source Credibility

The category of source perceptions that has received by far the most intensive research attention is source credibility. For more than two millennia, the term *ethos* was used to describe this group of perceptions. This view was drawn from the study of classical rhetoric, going all the way back to the fifth century B.C. at Syracuse in Sicily. The origin of the ethos concept is generally attributed to two Greek writers named Corax and Tisias (Sattler, 1947). *Source credibility*, on the other hand, is the term applied to the concept by early researchers in social psychology (Hovland, Janis, & Kelley, 1953). Because the ancients focused almost entirely on source credibility as the factor that determines the image of the speaker, their use of the term *ethos* was appropriate. However, we now recognize that there are many other important perceptions—all of which, when drawn together, form the ethos or image of the source in the receiver's mind.

Source credibility is the perception of a receiver that references the degree to which a source is seen as believable. Obviously, being seen as believable is a critical factor in the image of a teacher. If a student doesn't think he or she can believe what a teacher says, is there any reason to listen to that teacher at all? Not unless the student is required to take the course and pass the test created by the teacher! Thus, to the extent that any measure of freedom is permitted to the student, the teacher's source credibility is a determining factor for the student's selectivity.

The dimensionality of ethos or credibility has been the subject of extensive study. The results of the most recent research suggest there are three critical components of credibility. These are competence, trustworthiness, and goodwill.

Competence

Competence is the degree to which one is perceived to know what he or she is talking about. Terms that describe a competent person include "expert," "intelligent," "qualified," "knowledgeable," "educated," "experienced," and the like. A person we can describe in this way, then, may be seen as "believable" or "credible." On the other hand, people who might be described as "beginner," "ignorant," "uneducated," "unqualified," or "inexperienced" would not be seen as believable.

Trustworthiness

Trustworthiness is the degree to which one person is perceived as honest by another. Terms that describe a trustworthy person include "honest," "forthright," "good," "kind," "responsible," "decent," and having high character. A person who might be described in this way may also be seen as believable or credible. In contrast, people who might be described as "crooked," "dishonest," "bad," "unkind," "irresponsible," having low character, or being a liar would not be seen as trustworthy.

Perceptions of competence and trustworthiness have been found to vary independently of each other. That is, a teacher can be seen as high in both competence and trustworthiness, as high in competence but not trustworthy, as low in competence but highly trustworthy, or as low in both. To be seen as believable, however, the teacher must be seen as high in both competence and trustworthiness. If either competence or trustworthiness is seen as low or questionable, believability falls sharply.

Goodwill

The third dimension of credibility was named "goodwill" by Aristotle. Early researchers in social psychology referred to this dimension as "intent toward the receiver." For a considerable period of time—more than three decades—communication researchers disregarded this dimension, primarily because they had difficulty figuring out how to measure it. However, as a result of research in the area of communication in instruction, the importance of this dimension has once again been recognized. What Aristotle originally referenced as goodwill, instructional communication researchers have called "perceived caring." It is now recognized that these are the same thing (McCroskey & Teven, 1999; Teven & McCroskey, 1997).

This final category of credibility has received far less attention from researchers than those we will discuss later in this chapter, yet this may be the most important category of perceptions of all. Goodwill deals with how much the student perceives the teacher to be concerned about the student's welfare. Does the teacher see the student as a real person or as just another body filling up a seat? At the university level, this is sometimes discussed in terms of being seen as a "person" or as a "number," since in very large classes almost all records are handled numerically rather than on the basis of the "number"'s name.

The idea that the source's orientation toward the welfare of the receiver is important dates to antiquity. In Aristotle's work on ethos, he posited three components: intelligence, character, and goodwill. The first two components, competence and trustworthiness, are included in today's conceptualization of that construct. Goodwill was not found to be distinguishable from character in the early work on the measurement of ethos. Similarly, in the early work in social science on source credibility, three dimensions were posited: competence, trustworthiness, and intention toward the receiver. The first two were merged into the competence and character dimensions we discussed previously, while the intention dimension dropped by the wayside, probably because of measurement problems.

Both the goodwill and intention-toward-receiver conceptualizations are represented in the current "caring" construct. We are certainly going to listen more attentively to a person who we believe has our best interests at heart than to one who we think might be wanting to put one over on us. But the caring construct does not suggest that the opposite of caring is malicious intent; it is just indifference. Thus, the student won't automatically reject what the teacher says if that student is being treated as a number. Rather, such treatment will probably just make the student more suspicious of the teacher's motives. Teachers do not have to be devoted to their students for the students to learn. But if the teacher engages in behaviors that communicate goodwill and a positive intent to the students, they will probably try harder to learn what that teacher is trying to teach. It is believed that there are three factors that may lead students to perceive that the teacher has goodwill toward them and cares about their welfare: empathy, understanding, and responsiveness.

1. *Empathy.* Empathy is identification with another's feelings. Some teachers seem to be able to see instructional situations from the student's point of view, and others seem unable or unwilling to do so. Empathy is one of those "warm and fuzzy" concepts. While we have a hard time defining it or giving a good example of it, we know it when we see or feel it. When others not only can understand our view, but also can see the validity of the view, even if they do not agree with it, we feel closer to them. We think they care about us.

2. *Understanding.* Understanding is knowing another person's ideas, feelings, and needs. Some teachers seem almost intuitively to know what students think, when their feelings are hurt, when they have a problem, or what they need. Others seem to be insensitive to all of these things. Part of such understanding comes with experience, part from studying human psychology, and part from just being a keen observer of others' behavior. At any rate, when students see a teacher exhibiting understanding, they perceive that the teacher cares about them.

3. *Responsiveness.* Responsiveness is exhibited when a teacher reacts to student needs or problems quickly, when the teacher is attentive to the student, and when the teacher listens to what the student says. The responsive teacher recognizes and reacts to students, while the nonresponsive teacher's behavior is not modified in any significant way by students. The classic example of the nonresponsive teacher is the lecturer who stands behind a podium and reads a lecture to the students. The interactive teacher, on the other hand, adapts constantly to how the students are reacting to what he or she is saying. We perceive a person who responds to our communication as caring about us. Students view teachers in the same way.

Although we should not overemphasize the importance of goodwill in the instructional environment, it is important that we do not underemphasize it, either. There is a psychological closeness that develops between students and their teacher when the students perceive the teacher to be one who really cares about them. This kind of warm relationship is extremely supportive of learning and probably cannot be generated to the same extent in any other way.

The impact of caring on communication in instruction, and its role in source credibility, are both made clear in a quotation found on the bulletin board of a teachers' meeting room in a school in Martinsburg, West Virginia:

> "Students don't care about how much you know until they know about how much you care."

It probably is best if the teacher really cares about the student, but it is difficult for the teacher to care equally about all students. Thus, it is important that the teacher learn at least to exhibit behaviors consistent with caring. It is not the caring that is critical; it is the perceived caring. For the purposes of instruction, if you care but do not communicate that caring, you might as well not care at all.

Depending on the level of instruction, source credibility can be a given, or it can be difficult to achieve. Little children tend to believe adults, period. That is, they think all teachers know what they are talking about and are telling them the truth. As children get older, however, they become less universally trusting. By junior high school, many teachers are not seen as either competent or trustworthy. Competence perceptions are even more subject to question as the student progresses through higher levels of education. A perception that a teacher has very high character can even be taken as negative with older children and adults. A "goody-two-shoes" perception is not consistent with a perception of credibility, for it suggests being out of touch with reality, hence lower perceived competence. Even very small children appear to be sensitive to the fact that some adults—whether they are teachers or not—just don't care about them. This may prompt them to "act up" to get that person's attention, or they may simply try to avoid the person altogether.

At any level of instruction, a negative perception of the teacher on even one credibility dimension tends to destroy the teacher–student relationship. Teachers must protect their perceived credibility. They need to avoid obvious things such as lying to students or giving them information they are not certain is correct. Once a teacher's credibility is damaged, it may not be restored for a long time, if ever. Such concern, of course, increases according to teaching level, for older and more mature students may be more likely to observe flaws that young children may not. And although young children may forget things in a few days, older students are likely to remember for a lifetime violations related to any one of the credibility dimensions.

Temperament

The extensive research on source credibility has confirmed the existence of the three critical components of that category of source perceptions: competence, trustworthiness, and goodwill. In the process, three other perceptual dimensions were also isolated. Although these dimensions of perception were determined not to be components of credibility, they were found to be important to the overall images of sources. It is important, therefore, that teachers be aware of these perceptions. The perceptual dimensions have been found to be indicators of teachers' genetically based temperament and the way their temperament is typically manifested through communication. The labels that have been applied to these perceptions are composure, sociability, and extraversion.

Composure

The composure perception relates to the degree of emotional control a person is seen to have. This dimension is believed to be associated with the temperament variable known as *neuroticism.* Neurotic people typically are not composed.

Teachers must be able to control their emotions, or they invite challenge or even attack from verbally aggressive students. As one experienced junior high school teacher put it: "You never can let them know you aren't in control. They are like sharks. When they smell blood, they attack!" While the shark analogy may be a bit strong, it is often more apt than we would like. Substitute teachers, who often have a nebulous image at best, are apt to suffer from "shark attacks" when they appear nervous, shaken, or uncertain about what should be done next.

Of course, to be seen as in control of one's emotions is not the same as to be seen as having no emotions. When teachers try too hard to keep their emotions under wraps, they are likely to be seen as cold and aloof—a perception that puts off many students. Students are less likely to go to a cold, aloof teacher for help, even if they desperately need it.

Sociability

The sociability perception relates to the degree to which a person is seen as warm and friendly. It is believed that sociability is associated with the temperament variable known as *psychoticism*. Highly psychotic people are not sociable. A teacher who is perceived as sociable invites communication from students. Although this is generally a positive outcome, if a teacher has a very large class, being seen as sociable may invite more communication than she or he can handle. In the lower grades, however, being perceived as sociable is essential. At that level, much of the child's learning is a function of direct interaction with the teacher. Proportionately much less is learned at this level from books and other learning aids than at higher levels of instruction.

It is possible to be seen as too warm and friendly, particularly when the teacher and the students are not far apart in age. Students may see such teachers as pushovers. This can lead them to try to take advantage of the relationship. It is important that teachers distinguish clearly between "friendly" and "friend." While the former usually is positive, the latter often leads to trouble.

Extraversion

Extraversion refers to the degree to which a person is perceived as outgoing, active, and talkative. It is one of the three major temperament variables. People who are not extraverted are introverts. Teachers generally benefit from perceptions of moderately high extraversion. Those perceived to be low on extraversion are seen as withdrawn and uncommunicative. By contrast, those who are seen as very high in extraversion often are also seen as overly dominant and controlling. Sometimes the highly extraverted teacher can even create the stereotypical "used-car salesperson" image.

Teachers who generate perceptions of moderately high extraversion are likely to be seen as "with it." They often are perceived as people who know what they are doing and are on top of everything without being intrusive. They have control without being overly controlling.

Homophily

This category of perception concerns the degree to which a person sees someone else as similar to her- or himself. This perception is likely to have a major impact on both the initiation of communication and the effectiveness of that communication. The principle of homophily suggests that people who are more similar are more likely to attempt to communicate with one another and more likely to communicate effectively with one another, and, as a result of that communication, to become even more like one another. Thus, students who see their teacher as similar to themselves in important respects are likely to see that teacher as a model to emulate.

Research has identified several dimensions of homophily that may be important in the classroom context (McCroskey, Richmond, & Daly, 1975). These have been labeled demographic, background, and attitude.

Demographic Similarity

Demographics has to do with the characteristics of an individual compared with a population. People who are demographically similar may come from the same area—state, part of the state, county, city, or school—or they may be of the same sex, ethnic group, age group, sociological group, or economic group. The more of these demographic characteristics two people share, the more similar they are. Depending on the circumstances, however, one person may see another as highly similar even if the two people have only one demographic characteristic in common. A Caucasian American traveling in Asia for several weeks, for example, may see any other Caucasian whom he or she encounters as very similar, but would not see that person as similar at all "back home."

Students often see teachers as being very different from themselves. Although this is not always a bad thing, it can be very helpful to a teacher to have students who see her or him as at least somewhat like them demographically. Teachers students see as more demographically similar are more likely to be listened to than those seen as very different.

Background Similarity

Background similarity has to do with having similar experiences. This involves things like going to the same ball games, having the same hobbies, watching the same television shows, vacationing in the same area, going to the same stores, and the teacher having done some of the same things in the past that the student is doing now. Having the same experiences creates a feeling of sharing, of being alike, and it often increases teachers' empathy and responsiveness with students. If a student sees the teacher as having had similar experiences in the past, that greatly increases the value of the teacher's related opinions and advice.

Attitude Similarity

People who share beliefs, attitudes, and values or who otherwise think alike have attitude similarity. Since people normally believe that those who think the same way they do are wise, attitude similarity is probably the most important form of homophily. While it is unlikely that teachers and students will think alike on all issues, it is quite likely that they will share some attitudes. It is wise for the teacher to keep up with modern trends and fads, to know what is "in" with the younger crowd. If the teacher actually likes some of these things, making that known is likely to increase perceptions of attitude similarity. By contrast, pointing out how the teacher disagrees with students on other issues will reduce perceptions of attitude similarity.

Forms of similarity with teachers that are perceived by students provide an opportunity for improved communication with those students. The concept of optimum homophily is important here. A teacher is most influential with a student when the student sees the teacher as very much like her- or himself but also credits the teacher with knowing more about the topic of communication. At that point, the teacher can actually become an opinion leader for the student. This is a worthy goal for any teacher, but one not too often achieved, for an opinion leader is a person to whom another turns for advice or information or whose advice is respected if it is offered. The opinion leader–follower relationship is about as close to an ideal teacher–student relationship as one can achieve.

Interpersonal Attraction

Attraction, like credibility and homophily, is a multidimensional perception that one person can have of another person. We are drawn to people we find attractive in some way. We are most likely to initiate communication with those we find attractive, while we avoid communicating with people we find unattractive.

Research has identified three dimensions of attraction that may have an impact in instructional communication (McCroskey & McCain, 1974): physical, social, and task.

Physical Attraction

Physical attraction is often the first dimension of perception that has an impact on communication. It relates specifically to our view of someone in terms of her or his physical appearance. Our first reaction to another person is as an object. Although that object is a human being, we do not initially know the human characteristics of that individual. Hence, physical attraction is the single most important perception in initial communication encounters. In fact, if individuals do not find each other at least minimally physically attractive, it is probable there will be no communication between them at all.

It is popular in American culture to discount the importance of physical appearance. To present ourselves as egalitarian, we say things like "Beauty is in the eye of the beholder" and "Beauty is only skin deep." However, research indicates that we do not really act in accordance with those truisms. As some have put it, "Beauty may be only skin deep, but most people are only interested in skin!"

While physical attraction is an extremely powerful force that drives much human communication, it is of less importance when it comes to communication between teachers and students, for two reasons. First, this context only rarely involves any potential for sexual contact, even at the college level. As students become older, of course, sexual interests greatly increase, and the proverbial schoolgirl crush or its male equivalent can occur. Fortunately, the typical age gap between the teacher and the student reduces the likelihood of such interests developing. Most students are interested in people closer to their own age. Also, the cultural taboo against teacher–student romantic interest is very strong. Thus, even when crushes develop, they will usually end comparatively quickly, though often not as quickly as the teacher would prefer. Only if a teacher is particularly odd-looking is physical attraction a concern for children in elementary school.

Second, research has indicated that the impact of physical attraction is highest upon initial contact between people. As time goes on, its impact decreases sharply, and eventually the impact is virtually nil. Since teacher–student contact in the instructional environment normally is of a long-term nature—at least a term and often a year or more—whatever impact physical attraction has will wear off, and this perception may become quite irrelevant. Nevertheless, it is wise for teachers to make themselves at least moderately physically attractive, if possible, during the early days of contact with new students. But there's no need to despair just because one will never be confused with Ms. or Mr. America. That probably will not stand in the way of becoming an outstanding teacher.

Social Attraction

Social attraction refers to the degree to which one person perceives another person to be someone with whom he or she would like to spend time on a social or friendship level. It is desirable that the teacher be at least moderately socially attractive to the student, since this makes the learning environment more pleasant for the student. If the social attraction gets too strong, however, the student can become a pest by trying to be the teacher's pet.

Obviously, it is not appropriate under most circumstances for teachers and students to establish a social relationship apart from their instructional relationship. This can create role conflicts that may be difficult to deal with and that can lead both parties to have bad feelings toward each other over time. It is not uncommon for college instructors, particularly when they are young and are graduate assistants or beginning assistant professors, to establish social relationships with their students. Often their students are virtually the only people near their own age with whom they come into contact, and they would be lonely without such relationships. Unfortunately, if they are unable to maintain the appropriate status differential between themselves and their students, such relationships are likely to become very troublesome.

Task Attraction

Task attraction refers to the degree to which one person perceives it to be desirable to establish a work relationship with another person. This is the type of attraction that is critically important to positive teacher–student relationships.

If a student views the teacher as someone with whom it would be easy and pleasant to work, someone from whom he or she is likely to learn, and someone who is motivated to help students achieve their goals, this means the teacher is seen as task attractive by that student. When there is task attraction between teacher and student, it is likely their communication will be goal directed and quite effective.

Although it is possible for a student to perceive a teacher as highly attractive on all three of the attraction dimensions, it is not necessary for the teacher to be attractive on one dimension in order to be attractive on another. The only critical element in this context is task attraction, because it defines the relationship in the instructional setting. Hence, this is the dimension to which the teacher must give primary attention if he or she is to be effective.

We have centered our attention here on the attraction of students toward their teacher, but we should recognize that this is not the only context of attraction in the instructional environment. Most of students' attraction will be directed toward one another. Students' efforts to be physically and/or socially attractive to their peers can seriously interfere with the teacher's instructional efforts. Given the two, which do you think is more important to most students? If a teacher chooses to ignore or stifle these normal student behaviors, he or she can become extremely unattractive to students.

Attraction has serious implications for teachers who make use of group work in their instruction. If teachers assign students to groups, there will probably be students placed together who are not task attractive to one another. This may lead to little effort being put forth on the assigned project. On the other hand, if students are allowed to choose their own group project partners, such choices may be made more on physical or social grounds than on task grounds, particularly among middle and high school students. Although there is no simple solution to this problem, it is one to which teachers should attend in order to spot smaller problems before they become major ones.

Negative Images

Few teachers go out of their way to make themselves look bad. In fact, most teachers work hard to make themselves look good. Some work too hard and wind up with a negative image. Usually, in fact, the most negative images occur as a result of working too hard to produce a positive image on one or several of the dimensions of teacher image discussed earlier. That is, the teacher has worked on some dimensions while ignoring others. When this happens, what often is produced is a distorted image. When students focus primarily on one aspect of the teacher's image, it usually is seen as a negative one.

If you can figure out which images are being overemphasized in most of the following examples of teacher image labels, you probably have a good handle on this concept. Give it a try:

Everybody's buddy	Genius	Tough guy
Sensitive human being	Sex symbol	Grandmother
Taskmaster	Homeboy	Me too
Used-car salesperson	Chameleon	Ice cube
Deer in headlights	Mr. Warmth	Iron man

As you probably figured out as you went through these examples, more than one negative teacher image can be created by abuse of the same category of perceptions. It is important to remember that all of these perceptions are important to a first-rate teacher image. If we allow things to get out of balance, we will probably wind up with a negative image of one kind or another.

References

Brown, R. (1965). *Social psychology.* New York: Free Press.

Holtzman, P. D. (1966). Confirmation of ethos as a confounding element in communication research. *Speech Monographs, 30,* 464–466.

Hovland, C. I., Janis, I. L., & Kelley, H. H. (1953). *Communication and persuasion.* New Haven, CT: Yale University Press.

McCroskey, J. C., & Dunham, R. E. (1966). Ethos: A confounding element in communication research. *Speech Monographs, 30,* 456–463.

McCroskey, J. C., & McCain, T. A. (1974). The measurement of interpersonal attraction. *Speech Monographs, 20,* 261–266.

McCroskey, J. C., Richmond, V. P., and Daly, J. A. (1975). The measurement of perceived homophily in interpersonal communication. *Human Communication Research, 1,* 323–332.

McCroskey, J. C., & Teven, J. J. (1999). Goodwill: A re-examination of the construct and its measurement. *Communication Monographs, 66,* 90–103

McCroskey, J. C., & Young, T. J. (1981). Ethos and credibility: The construct and its measurement after three decades. *Central States Speech Journal, 32,* 24–34.

Sattler, W. M. (1947). Conceptions of ethos in ancient rhetoric. *Speech Monographs, 14,* 55–65.

Teven, J. J., & McCroskey, J. C. (1997). The relationship of perceived teacher caring with student learning and teacher evaluation. *Communication Education, 45,* 1–9.

Glossary

attitude similarity   Shared beliefs, attitudes, and values.

background similarity   Shared experiences relating to elements such as education, hobbies, sports interests, TV shows, and travel experiences.

competence   The degree to which a receiver perceives a source to be knowledgeable about what he or she is communicating.

composure (neuroticism)   The degree to which a receiver perceives that a source has emotional control when communicating.

demographic similarity   Shared characteristics related to elements such as sex, ethnic group, age group, sociological group, economic group, and geographics.

empathy   The degree to which a receiver perceives that a source can identify with her or his feelings.

ethos   The total image of a communication source in a receiver's mind.

extraversion   The degree to which a receiver perceives that a source is outgoing and willing to communicate with her or him.

goodwill   The degree to which a receiver perceives that a source has positive intentions toward her or him and cares about her or him.

opinion leader   A person to whom another turns in order to obtain information and/or guidance.

optimum homophily   Exists when one person sees her- or himself as very much like another but recognizes that the other is more knowledgeable about a given topic.

physical attraction   The degree to which one person desires to spend time with another person because he or she is perceived to have a positive physical appearance.

responsiveness   The degree to which a receiver perceives that a source listens to and is attentive to her or his communication.

social attraction   The degree to which one person desires to spend time with another to engage in social activities.

sociability (psychoticism)   The degree to which a receiver perceives that a source is friendly and cooperative.

source credibility   The degree to which a receiver perceives a source to be believable.

sponsorship effect   When an unknown source is introduced to receivers, a portion of the introducer's ethos is transferred to the unknown source.

task attraction   The degree to which one person desires to spend time with another to engage in work activities.

temperament   Genetically based supertraits that are related to many personality variables.

trustworthiness   The degree to which a receiver perceives that a source will tell the truth about what he or she knows.

understanding   The degree to which a receiver perceives that a source understands her/his ideas, feelings, and needs.

8

Power in the Classroom

Power, as we will use the term in this chapter, refers to an individual's ability to have an effect on the behavior of another person or group. It is important, therefore, that a teacher have power in the instructional environment so that he or she can influence the behavior of students so they will learn the content of the subject matter being taught.

While most teachers, and most students, who read this assessment of power will agree with it, some people will not. They may have an image of power as something highly destructive and evil, like the power to blow up the world. We are not talking about that kind of power here; atomic weapons are beyond the control of teachers—and (fortunately) students also. We are looking at power as the ability to help students learn, not as a capacity to force others to do what we want them to.

Power in the instructional environment must be granted to the teacher by the student. No teacher has power over the behavior of a student unless the student agrees to it. The power of the grade is impotent for the student who does not care about the grade. The power of expulsion is impotent for the student who does not want to be in school. The power of the paddle is impotent for the student in a contest with another student for how many "whacks" they can accumulate. The power of candy is impotent for the student who does not like candy. And the power of your praise is impotent for the student who does not care what you think.

Power and student affect for the teacher and subject matter are highly interrelated. Students who like the teacher are more likely to do what the teacher asks. Students who like the subject matter also are more likely to do what the teacher asks. Power improperly used will destroy affect in the classroom. It will lead the student to dislike the teacher and dislike the subject taught as well. Teachers can make no more serious error than to abuse their power with their students. The basic principle of power is: To abuse it is to lose it.

Bases of Power

The nature of power has been the subject of hundreds of treatises in the social sciences and humanities over the past century. To say scholars have been fascinated with power is an understatement. The work of French and Raven (1959) has had a particularly strong influence in the field of communication. These authors advanced a conceptualization of the bases of power that has been expanded upon and used as a foundation for research relating to communication in instruction (McCroskey & Richmond, 1983; Richmond & McCroskey, 1984; Richmond & Roach, 1992). It is useful for us to examine French and Raven's thinking with particular application to the instructional setting. They suggested that there are five bases of power in human relations: assigned, coercive, reward, expert, and referent.

Assigned Power

Assigned power, sometimes referred to as legitimate power, is presumed to be given to an individual as a function of her or his title or position. It comes as a function of the person's role in a system. A person with the title "teacher" is presumed by most to have been assigned the duty (and right) to check the attendance of students in her or his class. A person appointed to the position of "principal" is presumed by most to have the authority to supervise the behavior of students (and teachers) in the school building.

Although the system operates as if these assigned powers and duties are legitimate, individuals may not accept them as legitimate. If a female student refuses to "walk in the hall" (instead of running), even though the principal tells her to do so, she has effectively rejected the assigned power of the principal. At this point, the principal must decide whether to accept her refusal and allow the student to do as she wants or move on to another basis of power to try to influence her behavior. It is most important to realize that, although the system can assign the title or position, only the student can grant the power presumably assigned by the system. If the student does not consider power legitimate, for all intents and purposes, it isn't.

Coercive Power

Coercive power is the power to punish and/or to threaten to punish. Teachers have a certain number of punishments at their disposal. These include lowering grades, eliminating recess, restricting attendance at special classes, ejecting students from class, assigning detention, suspension, expulsion, corporal punishment, and so on. Sometimes these things need only be suggested in order to obtain compliance with the teacher's demands. Sometimes, in fact, just the student's knowledge that these punishments could be carried out, or merely threatened, is enough to produce compliance.

On the other hand, coercive power provides the best example of how power must be granted by the student. Getting it from the system is not necessarily enough. If the punishments available are not threatening to the given student, the coercive power of the teacher is nil. Even such extreme penalties as corporal punishment are totally ineffective for some students. They may even get involved in games where in order to win, they must be subjected to corporal punishment by the teacher or principal. As one teacher commented facetiously during a discussion of the effectiveness of corporal punishment, "Corporal punishment is worthless; until we have capital punishment, we have no punishment at all!"

The teacher's point is well taken. Coercion works only if the punishment to which the teacher has access is something the student really wants to avoid. Sometimes it takes great creativity on the part of the teacher and/or the principal to identify a consequence that would be seen as a punishment by a given student. And from an educational perspective, punishment is something that probably should be avoided when possible. If a student must be punished to learn, exactly what is it that the student is learning? Sometimes that is difficult to know.

It is often said that punishment simply "does not work." This conclusion is sometimes drawn from an inadequate reading of research on learning. That research indicates that punishment can work, but only under highly constrained circumstances. Most important, if punishment is to be used, it must be used immediately after the inappropriate behavior is performed. Otherwise, the punishment will have an impact only on the receiver's attitudes toward the person delivering the punishment, not on the behavior for which the punishment was intended. A classic example is the stereotypical threat issued by the mother who says, "Wait till Dad gets home!" If that approach is used often enough, it will not correct any particular behavior of the child, but it may cause the child to fear the father, even when there has been no misbehavior. The same principle applies to the teacher who uses the principal as the "bogeyman."

Although punishment itself, particularly corporal punishment, is generally ineffective, the threat of punishment is often highly effective. For coercion to be effective, however, three conditions must be met: The student must be aware that there is concern, control, and scrutiny.

1. *Concern.* The student must believe the teacher cares whether or not he or she complies with the request. Often, rules are made, but no one seems to care if they are broken. This is particularly true of rules that are made above the teacher's head, and that the teacher does not like. Some examples of such "soft rules" outside the school environment are laws against speeding and possession of marijuana in some areas. Both are against the law, but the fine for violation may be as little as $5.00. Everyone understands that most people feel there must be laws against these behaviors, but no one really expects people to follow these laws. Many schools have these kinds of rules: no gum chewing, no kissing in the hallways, and so on. Although in some places these rules are not only made but also stringently enforced, in other places no one really cares, so students do not follow them.

2. *Control.* The student must believe the teacher can actually administer the threatened punishment. Exaggerated threats ("You will stay in detention until you die!") will be ignored. Authority to deliver even minimal punishment must be in place. Unless there is a record of the principal backing up the teacher, all threats will be meaningless.

At one university with which we are familiar, a student was found innocent on a charge of cheating despite direct, physical evidence that the student did, in fact, cheat. The faculty review committee decided that because the teacher had not specifically told the student that he could not copy his work out of a published work written by someone else, he could not be held responsible. Even though such plagiarism was clearly described in the student handbook as unacceptable, the committee did not hold the student responsible for reading the handbook. After that incident, there was very little the faculty could do to threaten students for cheating—and the students knew it.

3. *Scrutiny.* The student must believe that the teacher will know if a rule is broken. In short, he or she must not believe the rule can be broken when the teacher "is not looking." When scrutiny is doubtful, violating the rule may become a game—for example, chewing on one's gum only when the teacher is looking at the other side of the room. The importance of this condition has been recognized by quite a few police departments. In several areas, empty police cars are parked along the roadway to reduce speeding. Indeed, speeding motorists quickly slow down when they see the police car, because they believe they are being scrutinized. Of course, when they see that the car is empty, they speed up again. Some particularly devious officers went one better than this: They parked an empty police car by the roadside, then manned a radar trap a couple of miles down the road. The motorists slowed down for the empty car and increased their speed again just in time to get caught in the trap!

If punishment is to be used effectively in the classroom, it cannot be allowed to become a game. Punishment should be administered every time a violation occurs (particularly when the rule is first imposed or the relationship between the teacher and the student is new), the severity of the punishment should not vary, and it should be administered as soon as possible after the violation. When this system is followed, it communicates concern, control, and scrutiny; and, most important, it will work. Unfortunately, it is comparatively rare that this system can be followed. It is usually impossible to know every time a violation occurs. As a result, the effectiveness of coercive power in the classroom is generally very low.

Reward Power

There are two general categories of rewards—extrinsic and intrinsic—and their nature and impact are quite different. Extrinsic rewards are tangible items—candy, bonus points toward a grade, extra recess, permission to do something the student enjoys. Such rewards are particularly useful for short-term effects. Concern, control, and scrutiny are also critical to the effective use of extrinsic reward. The student has to believe the teacher cares whether he or she engages in the desired behavior. As with punishment, at first, extrinsic rewards should be administered every time the desired behavior occurs, although it will not be necessary to provide such continuous rewards as time passes and the student's behavior becomes habitual. Similarly, the student must believe that the teacher has the power to give the reward and will know when the student engages in the desired behavior.

Reward of the extrinsic type, though it has a far better reputation, is just the flip side of coercion. Coercion (punishment) is the stick; reward is the carrot. Both are controlling mechanisms, and neither is more "moral" than the other. But most students would rather be controlled by the carrot than by the stick! Using extrinsic rewards will tend to enhance positive teacher–student relationships, if they have any effect at all, whereas use of punishment will tend to destroy those relationships.

The major problem with the use of extrinsic rewards is that the teacher who depends too heavily on this type of power may find that he or she has run out of "goodies." After a while, students take extrinsic rewards for granted as a right. Then the "what have you done for me lately" mind-set may take over. Each time extrinsic rewards are used as a bribe for desired behavior, the stakes for that behavior increase. Eventually, the teacher has to run out of goodies. When that happens, the behavior stops, because it is not based on the student's positive orientation toward the behavior itself.

The second type of reward is intrinsic reward. These can be intangible things like praise, a warm touch, a smile, the pleasure of learning, the discovery of new ideas, or the opportunity to succeed. When this type of reward comes from learning the content itself, it is independent of the teacher. Thus, it is not so much the power of the teacher as it is the voluntary choice of the student that produces the desired reward for the behavior. When the intrinsic reward is delivered by the teacher (such as praise, a touch, a smile), its effect depends in large measure on the teacher's expert or referent power. We will discuss these as separate bases of power later in the chapter.

Although intrinsic reward is not a separate base of power for the teacher, it has an important impact on students. Intrinsic reward has been shown in many studies to be much more effective than extrinsic reward for producing long-term behavior effects (those that continue when the teacher is no longer present). A classic study illustrates the effects of the two. Two groups of children were placed in rooms with Tinker Toys. Both played with the toys. One group was praised (intrinsic reward) for what they built, while the other group was given candy (extrinsic reward) for their work. Each group was then taken to another room in which a wide variety of toys were available. The children in the group that received praise chose to play with Tinker Toys again. The children in the group that received candy chose other toys instead. Given the regularity with which these sorts of results have been observed, it is clear that intrinsic reward is the more powerful type.

The teacher needs to understand the principle of equity if he or she is to employ either type of reward. According to this principle, inputs should equal outputs. What this means in this context is that students expect that the reward will be equal to the effort and the effort will be equal to the reward. Thus, if a student works hard, he or she believes the reward for that work should be high. Hence, it is not unusual for the student who has worked hard to expect a high grade even if the quality of the work is poor. Similarly, students who expend little effort are not likely to expect much reward. Some students, for example, are quite happy with a C because they do not want to work hard enough to earn an A or B.

When the student's expectations for equity are not met, there may be a problem. Students who are graded down because the teacher feels they are not working up to their potential may feel cheated. In this case, their reward did not equal their effort, so the result is anger. In the future, these students may not be willing to expend even as much effort as they did previously. By contrast, when the reward is higher than expected—when the student receives an A even though he or she has exerted only enough effort to warrant a C—the effort does not equal the reward, so the result is guilt. This may cause the student to devalue the reward by degrading the course as a "Mickey Mouse" class. This, then, would justify the high reward received for so little effort.

Problems of inequity often result when teachers are not sensitive to what their reward-oriented behaviors are communicating. It is important to recognize that rewards are messages sent by a source (the teacher) to a receiver (the student). The meaning of those messages, as with all other messages, is determined by the student. Being sensitive to feedback from students with regard to reward can be valuable in adapting rewards to be more appropriate for each student.

Expert Power

Expert power represents the power of information. Students generally respect knowledge. A teacher's ability to control student behavior increases as a function of the students' belief that the teacher is competent and knowledgeable. Students are more likely to do homework if they believe their teacher is an expert than if they do not believe the teacher knows what he or she is talking about.

Younger children, of course, tend to think all adults are experts—on everything. But as they get a bit older, they begin to recognize that not all adults are equal, and some of them are not too bright. By the time they reach middle or junior high school, they are likely to be suspicious of their teachers' expertise. Thus, except when working with very young children, the teacher's expert power must be earned with each class of students he or she teaches.

Referent Power

Referent power is the power of association. The degree to which students like, admire, and respect the teacher as a person influences her or his power to control student behavior. Students want to emulate and model teachers who have high referent power. They want to be around such teachers, do what they do, and be like them "when they grow up."

As is the case with expert power, teachers of younger children typically have a relatively high degree of referent power. The little ones want to be with the teacher, sit on the teacher's lap, get a hug from the teacher, and so on. As they get older, they are less willing to view any given teacher as a role model.

Sources of Power

There are two sources of power. Some power is perceived to be derived as a function of the organization in which one works. Other power is derived from personal relationships.

Organizational Power

Organizations select their representatives and legitimatize them with appropriate titles. They also provide them with the authority to dispense certain punishments and extrinsic rewards on behalf of the organization. School systems are organizations. A school system's representatives are the teachers and the administrators. Students who want to be in the system and sanctioned by the system (to pass to the next grade or graduate, for example), then, must accept the "authority" given the teachers and administrators. Those who do not can reject that authority, but those who want to earn the rewards or to avoid the punishments must accept the authority delegated by the organization. Those who do not care about the rewards and who can tolerate the available punishments can reject that authority.

Organizational power is very strong at the elementary and secondary levels of education. Even if the students do not care at all about learning anything, most of them, by law, cannot just quit school. But even though the law can force students to go to school, it cannot force them to like it. Thus, if a student rejects the authority of the school and cares nothing about the rewards the teachers have to offer, the only organizational power remaining is punishment. Some students will even be willing to accept all the punishment the system can throw at them, because what they want most is the ultimate punishment—expulsion. Thus, even though organizational power can force a student to be present, it is in no position to guarantee learning. Students will learn if they choose to do so, and organizational power alone cannot force that choice.

Personal Power

Because of the limitations of organizational power, the real power that counts in organizations is personal power. Personal power is based on relationships between people. In a school system, teachers generate power through positive relationships with students. Positive relationships permit the teacher to exercise referent and expert power and, as a function of these bases of power, provide extrinsic rewards to students. As long as the teacher and the students agree to maintain such a positive relationship, this power continues to exist. When such a relationship ends, the personal power of the teacher ends, and the only remaining means of controlling student behavior comes from organizational power.

Teacher power exists only if the student permits it to exist. It is critical that the teacher develop relationships with students that lead to the acceptance of teacher power in the classroom. When the teacher must wage a constant struggle for power, he or she has little opportunity to enhance student learning. Students benefit the most from their educational experience when they have strong personal relationships with their teachers. Why this is the case is best illustrated through an examination of the levels of influence that are possible in the classroom.

Levels of Influence

Teachers seek to influence students, but not every influence achieved is of equal consequence. As Kelman (1961) has noted, influence has a depth component. Some influence is transitory, while some is much more long-lasting. Some influence represents achievement of very important instructional goals, but some reflects nothing more than necessary student cooperation. Different levels of influence may require the use of different bases of power to achieve. We will consider three major levels of influence: compliance, identification, and internalization.

Compliance

Compliance is the most transitory level of influence. The teacher is not primarily concerned with whether the behavior will be continued over any significant period of time. He or she just wants it to occur when it is asked for. The motto for this level of influence is "Just do it." It is not required that the students like it or even that they do it when the teacher is not around, just that they do it when the teacher is present.

This is the level of influence that is expected for most ordinary classroom rules—not chewing gum, raising one's hand and being called on before speaking, getting in line before leaving the room, turning in homework on time, not hitting other students over the head, and so on. The bases of power for gaining compliance are generally thought to be the legitimate, coercive, and reward bases, because these are the bases brought into play when such rules are broken. However, expert and referent power often lead students to comply with rules without the teacher even being aware it is happening, much less making a special effort to ensure compliance.

Identification

The motto for this level of influence is "It's a good idea." This is a more lasting level of influence. The student understands why the behavior is recommended or required, thinks it is a good idea, and most likely engages in it even when the teacher is not present. When confronted with a choice, the student chooses the desired behavior. The student comes to identify with the behavior, sometimes to the point where he or she will even attempt to persuade other students to engage in the behavior.

Although students may enter a class with a new teacher who is already identified with the given behavior, it is unlikely that the teacher will gain such identification from the legitimate, coercive, or reward power bases. In the absence of expert and/or referent power, the teacher is unlikely to produce this level of influence. The fact that a disliked teacher approves of some behavior is usually enough to make the students dislike that behavior.

Internalization

This is the most lasting level of influence. The motto for this level is "It's a habit." The student no longer thinks about whether to engage in the given behavior. It is fully accepted that the behavior is appropriate, so no conscious decision is even being made by the student. Because the behavior is a habituated reaction of the student, it occurs in all appropriate conditions. It is a part of the student's normal behavioral repertoire.

It is this level of influence that society has in mind when it agrees to pay for schools and teachers to "civilize and educate" its children. This level of influence is not produced by legitimate, coercive, or reward power bases. It is virtually impossible to achieve this level of influence without expert and referent power.

The importance of understanding the levels of influence stems from the relationship between level of influence and instructional goals. While short-term behavior change (compliance) can be achieved through any of the power bases, long-term change comes only from referent and/or expert power bases. Thus, teachers must develop and maintain positive relationships with students if they are to have any hope of accomplishing the larger objectives of instruction. When the primary focus is placed on short-term objectives such as basic behavioral compliance with school rules and mastering low-level cognitive objectives, the real goals of instruction may be sacrificed. It is important that, when using power in the classroom, teachers realize they must weigh the costs of obtaining low-level behavioral compliance against the benefits of achieving long-term goals of instruction.

Balancing Costs and Benefits

Teachers begin with a limited amount of power in the classroom. The power that stems from the organization is generally seen by students as antisocial, and many will resist it. Resorting to the use of organizational power can seriously damage the relationship between the teacher and the students, leaving the teacher virtually powerless. Under such circumstances, physical control and punishment become the only control mechanisms available, rather than being the choices of last resort.

The teacher who builds strong positive relationships with students builds a strong prosocial power base and reduces the need to use antisocial control methods. Several considerations should be kept in mind by the teacher who wants to function in this way.

Determine the Absolutes

Rules must be established for appropriate student behavior. However, every rule established provides another possibility for conflict between teacher and student. Hence, the general guideline is to establish only those rules that are absolutely necessary. The teacher must decide what must be done and must not be done. Beyond those absolutes, he or she should refrain from establishing many more rules.

Perceive the Possible

It is not reasonable to expect students to behave in an ideal manner at all times. A certain amount of acting up is virtually guaranteed. To try to control every aspect of any human's behavior is best left to prison authorities. Such attempts have no place in schools. Some latitude must be provided students or they will rebel against the system. The teacher must target the possible, not the ideal. Otherwise, her or his communication will result in personal rejection by the students.

Determine What Is Worth Sacrificing For

Some rules are more important than others. Some misbehaviors are more serious than others. The prosocial power bases lead to prevention of misbehavior. Thus, only the antisocial power bases are readily available to correct students for misbehavior. Such corrections are likely to make the teacher–student relationship less positive, so the teacher must decide what problems really justify sacrificing the relationship with the student.

Know When to Avoid Confrontation

It is best to avoid confrontations with students—especially in front of other students, teachers, or parents. It is difficult for a student to back down in front of others, even if the student knows he or she is in the wrong. Consequently, interactions with students that have the potential for confrontation should be conducted in private. This permits the student to submit to the teacher's requests without losing face. Some teachers want to confront students in front of other students so they can make an example out of them. *Remember: Making an example of a student is making an enemy of a student.* And often, making an example of the student is making a fool of the teacher!

Win by Losing Gracefully

As much as we might want it to be otherwise, sometimes the teacher is in the wrong. Winning by refusing to acknowledge errors, or demanding and obtaining compliance in such circumstances, is losing—and losing big. It is important in students' minds that the teacher be a fair person. Taking advantage of the organizational power in the relationship with the student will seriously damage that relationship and will reduce personal power not only with that student but also with other students who observe that happening or who hear about it later. Admitting error is a sign of maturity, one that will help earn the respect of students, not lose it.

It is important for teachers to realize that they are the only mature person in most of their interactions with students, at least at the elementary and secondary levels. It should not surprise them that students behave in an immature manner. Since someone needs to behave in a calm, mature manner, it is incumbent on the teacher to be that someone.

Behavioral Alteration Techniques and Messages

When we say a teacher "uses" one base of power or another, the unstated fact is that the teacher somehow communicates with the student to draw upon that power. Sometimes that use of power is direct ("If you do not follow the rule, you will not be allowed out for recess"), and sometimes it is quite indirect (the teacher smiles at the student and asks her or him to close the door). In any event, power and communication are intertwined.

An extensive series of research studies was conducted in the 1980s and early 1990s (citations for these are included in the references at the end of this chapter) that sought to identify the techniques teachers actually employ to exert power in the classroom and the kinds of communicative messages that represent those efforts. The techniques were referred to as Behavior Alteration Techniques (BATs), and the messages were referred to as Behavior Alteration Messages (BAMs). Figure 8.1 presents a list of the resulting 22 BAT categories and representative examples of BAMs for each category.

This research began with the French and Raven (1959) bases of power already discussed. As the research developed, the nature of these bases was widened somewhat, and at least two more bases became evident. We will discuss the seven bases (and 22 BATs) here to indicate the much wider choice of options available for teachers than was initially apparent. While all of the BATs were easily recognizable to many of the teachers studied, the research indicated that most teachers reported using only a half dozen or so. Interactions with the teachers indicated that the reason they used only a limited variety of techniques was most often that the individual teacher was not aware of other possibilities. It is our belief that the more options teachers are aware of, the more likely they are to choose an option that will work without negative side effects.

Reward

The first five BATs fall in this category. You will recognize that this category is much broader than the original reward category discussed earlier in this chapter. The present category includes not only rewards that may come from the teacher but also rewards that come from the behavior itself (both immediate and deferred), from people other than the teacher, and from the student's internal feelings (self-esteem).

1. *Immediate Reward from Behavior.* You will enjoy it. It will make you happy. Because it is fun. You will find it rewarding/ interesting. It is a good experience.
2. *Deferred Reward from Behavior.* It will help you later on in life. It will prepare you for getting a job (or going to graduate school). It will prepare you for achievement tests (or the final exam). It will help you with upcoming assignments.
3. *Reward from Teacher.* I will give you a reward if you do. I will make it beneficial for you. I will give you a good grade (or extra credit) if you do. I will make you my assistant.
4. *Reward from Others.* Others will respect you if you do. Others will be proud of you. Your friends will like you if you do. Your parents will be pleased.
5. *Self-Esteem.* You will feel good about yourself if you do. You are the best person to do it. You always do such a good job.
6. *Punishment from Behavior.* You will lose if you don't. You will be unhappy if you don't. You will be hurt if you don't. It's your loss. You'll feel bad if you don't.
7. *Punishment from Teacher.* I will punish you if you don't. I will make things miserable for you. I'll give you an "F" if you don't. If you don't do it now, it will be homework later.
8. *Punishment from Others.* No one will like you. Your friends will make fun of you. Your parents will punish you if you don't. Your classmates will reject you.
9. *Guilt.* If you don't, others will be hurt. You'll make others unhappy if you don't. Your parents will feel bad if you don't. Others (e.g., classmates, friends) will be punished if you don't.
10. *Teacher/Student Relationship: Positive.* I will like you better if you do. I will respect you. I will think more highly of you. I will appreciate you more if you do. I will be proud of you and supportive of you.
11. *Teacher/Student Relationship: Negative.* I will dislike you if you don't. I will lose respect for you if you don't. I will think less of you if you don't. I won't be proud of you. I'll be disappointed in you.
12. *Legitimate–Higher Authority.* Do it. I'm telling you what I was told. It is a rule. I have to follow it and so do you. It's administrative/school policy.

Continued

FIGURE 8.1 *Behavioral Alteration Techniques and Messages*

Figure 8.1 *Continued*

13. *Legitimate: Teacher Authority.* Because I told you so. You don't have a choice. You're here to work. I'm the teacher, you're the student. I'm in charge/control, not you. Don't ask, just do it.
14. *Personal (Student) Responsibility.* It is your obligation. It is your turn. Everyone has to do his/her share. It's your job. Everyone has to pull his/her own weight.
15. *Responsibility to Class.* Your group needs it done. The class is depending on you. All your friends are counting on you. Don't let your group down. You'll ruin things for the rest of the class. It's your responsibility.
16. *Normative Rules.* The majority rules. All your friends are doing It. Everyone else has to do It. The rest of the class is doing it. It's part of growing up.
17. *Debt.* You owe me one. Pay your debt. You promised to do it. I did it the last time. You said you'd try to do it this time.
18. *Altruism.* If you do this, it will help others. Others will benefit if you do. It will make others happy if you do. I'm not asking you to do it for yourself; do it for the good of your classmates and friends.
19. *Peer Modeling.* Your friends do it. Classmates you respect do it. The friends you admire are doing it. Other students you like do it. All your friends are doing it.
20. *Teacher Modeling.* This is the way I always do it. When I was your age, I did it. People who are like me do it. I had to do this when I was in school. Teachers you like and respect do it.
21. *Expert Teacher.* From my experience, it is a good idea. From what I have learned, it is what you should do. This has always worked for me. Trust me–I know what I'm doing. I had to do this before I became a teacher.
22. *Teacher Responsiveness (formerly teacher feedback).* Because I need to know how well you understand this. To see how well I've taught you. To see how well you can do it. It will help me know your problem areas.

All of the BATs have been found to be generally neutral or slightly positively related to student learning, both cognitive and affective. Thus, these BATs may be used, at least in moderation, with reasonable confidence that they will do no harm. Since BATs are used primarily to control student behavior, this is a very important concern. We should not expect methods of control to make students learn more cognitively or develop more positive affect for the teacher or the subject matter. We can, however, reasonably hope to find methods of control that do not reduce learning. The BATs in this category appear to do just that.

Punishment

BATs 6–9 fall in this category. Like the reward category, it is an expansion of one of the earlier categories (coercion). The present category includes not only punishments that may be imposed by the teacher but also punishments that come from the behavior itself, from people other than the teacher, and from the student's internal feelings (guilt).

All of these BATs have been found to be negatively associated with affective learning, and "punishment from teacher" and "from behavior" have been found to be negatively associated with cognitive learning and motivation as well. Clearly, BATs in this category should be resorted to only when others with less likelihood of doing damage have not been effective.

Relational

The two BATs (10 and 11) in this category are alike in that they both deal with the teacher–student relationship. However, the impact of the two has been found to be very different. The positive use of the relationship has been found to have a neutral impact on learning, but the negative use has been found to have a negative impact on learning and motivation.

Legitimate

BATs 12 and 13 compose this category. Number 12 relates to a higher authority; number 13 relates to one's own authority. Both should be avoided. The research indicates that both have a negative impact on both cognitive and affective learning and that they tend to reduce student motivation.

Moral Responsibility

BATs 14–18 are included in this category. Of these, only "debt" poses problems for the teacher. Drawing on debt tends to reduce affect for both the teacher and the subject matter. By contrast, personal responsibility, responsibility to the class, normative rules, and altruism appear to be neutral in their impact on learning and motivation. This category represents a fertile source of techniques for influencing students, although extremely high use of such methods might cause resentment over time.

Referent

Peer and teacher modeling BATs compose this category. The research seems to suggest that the BATs in this category are probably best used in an indirect manner. If used in moderation, however, these BATs are not likely to have any meaningful negative impact on learning or motivation, even when used directly. It should be recognized that referent power probably has its most positive effect when its presence is not overly emphasized.

Expert

The final category includes the final two BATs, numbers 21 and 22. Both allude to the expertness of the teacher. As with the BATs in the referent category, the research seems to suggest that these BATs are probably best used in an indirect manner, although it is unlikely that the teacher-responsiveness BAT will result in any negative response even if it is used very directly.

On balance, of these 22 BATs, the majority (15) can be used with confidence that they will not only help control and direct student behavior but also avoid damaging the students' learning or motivation. BATs 6–9 and 11–13 should be reserved for use only in emergencies . These are the BATs that primarily represent coercive and legitimate power, along with the debt BAT from the moral-responsibility category.

The most important thing we can learn from the contemporary research on power in the classroom is that it is very possible to control and direct the behavior of the overwhelming majority of students without resorting to antisocial methods. However, if a teacher develops a negative relationship with a student or a group of students, most of the prosocial methods for control are lost, leaving only the antisocial. It is critical, therefore, that teachers make a concerted effort to build positive teacher–student relationships in order to prevent problems. Many of the communication issues discussed in this book, and the others in this series, are specifically directed toward accomplishing that objective.

References

French, J. R. P. Jr., & Raven, B. (1959). The bases for social power. In D. Cartwright (Ed.), *Studies in social power* (pp. 150–167). Ann Arbor, MI: Institute for Social Research.

Kearney, P., Plax, T. G., Richmond, V. P., & McCroskey, J. C. (1984). Power in the classroom IV: Alternatives to discipline. In R. Bostrom (Ed.), *Communication yearbook 8* (pp. 724–746). Beverly Hills, CA: Sage.

Kearney, P., Plax, T. G., Richmond, V. P., & McCroskey, J. C. (1985). Power in the classroom III: Teacher communication techniques and messages. *Communication Education, 34,* 19–28.

Kelman, H. C. (1961). Processes of opinion change. *Public Opinion Quarterly, 25,* 58–78.

McCroskey, J. C., & Richmond, V. P. (1983). Power in the classroom I: Teacher and student perceptions. *Communication Education, 32,* 175–184.

McCroskey, J. C., Richmond, V. P., Plax, T. G., & Kearney, P. (1985). Power in the classroom V: Behavior alteration techniques, communication training, and learning. *Communication Education, 34,* 214–226.

Plax, T. G., & Kearney, P. (1992). Teacher power in the classroom: Defining and advancing a program of research. In V. P. Richmond & J. C. McCroskey (Eds.), *Power in the classroom: Communication, control, and concern* (pp. 67–84). Hillsdale, NJ: Lawrence Erlbaum Associates.

Plax, T. G., Kearney, P., McCroskey, J. C., & Richmond, V. P. (1986). Power in the classroom VI: Verbal control strategies, nonverbal immediacy, and affective learning. *Communication Education, 35,* 43–55.

Richmond, V. P. (1990). Communication in the classroom: Power and motivation. *Communication Education, 39,* 181–195.

Richmond, V. P., & McCroskey, J. C. (1984). Power in the classroom II: Power and learning. *Communication Education, 33,* 125–136.

Richmond, V. P., McCroskey, J. C., Kearney, P., & Plax, T. G. (1987). Power in the classroom VII: Linking behavior alteration techniques to cognitive learning. *Communication Education, 36*, 1–12.

Richmond, V. P., & Roach, K. D. (1992). Power in the classroom: Seminal studies. In V. P. Richmond & J. C. McCroskey (Eds.), *Power in the classroom: Communication, control, and concern* (pp. 47–65). Hillsdale, NJ: Lawrence Erlbaum Associates.

Glossary

assigned power (legitimate)   Power based on the title and job description given to the individual by an organization.

behavior alteration messages   Communicative messages that reflect different kinds of influence strategies.

behavior alteration techniques   Communication strategies designed to influence others.

coercive power   Power based on the authority of the organization given to an individual to threaten or punish another person.

compliance   Engaging in a required/requested behavior while under the supervision of another.

concern   An individual believes that the person exerting coercion or reward cares whether he or she engages in the behavior required.

control   An individual believes that the person exerting coercion or reward can deliver the threatened punishment or promised reward.

expert power   The person is granted power because he/she is believed to know a great deal about the situation of concern.

identification   Engaging in a required/requested behavior because the individual believes it is the appropriate behavior.

internalization   Engaging in a required/requested behavior because it has been habituated.

organizational power   Power that presumably is granted an individual by the organization as a part of the job (assigned, coercive, reward).

personal power   Power that is generated by the individual through positive relationships with others (expert, referent).

power   The ability of one person to have an effect on the behavior of another person or group.

referent power   The person is granted power because he/she is accepted as a role model.

reward power   Power based on the authority of the organization given to an individual to promise or provide a reward to another person.

scrutiny   An individual believes that the person exerting coercion or reward will be able to know whether he/she engages in the behavior required.

9

Expectancies, Grouping, and Classroom Communication

We indicated in Chapter 6 that expectancies can have a major impact on the way we selectively perceive messages. Such perceptions, in turn, have a major impact on our communication behavior. *Expectancies are merely our predictions of future occurrences—what we anticipate will happen.* Our biased, unjustified evaluations often influence our expectancies. We all have expectancies. They cannot be completely avoided, no matter how hard we try. But if we can recognize our expectancies and where they come from, we may be able to limit their negative impact. Many believe that the most serious problem that stems from these expectancies is the problem of self-fulfilling prophecies.

Self-Fulfilling Prophecies

A self-fulfilling prophecy is an expectancy effect. It is a prophecy that comes true in part because one expects it to come true. When we think something will happen, we sometimes do things, usually unconsciously, to cause it to happen. If our behavior is called to our attention, we may be surprised to learn we had such an effect. Sometimes, people are even unwilling to admit that they did what was observed, particularly if bias may have been a factor in the behavior.

The classic example of how this can happen in a classroom was reported in the book *Pygmalion in the Classroom* (Rosenthal & Jacobson, 1968). A study was conducted in which elementary school teachers' expectancies about some of their students were manipulated in a way that was intended to be beneficial to those students. The teachers were led to believe that some of their students were "late bloomers" but that these students would achieve at an accelerated pace sometime soon after the beginning of the school year. Actually, these so-called late bloomers were simply students of average to below-average intelligence who had been randomly selected from the students in the classes studied. In short, no valid method whatsoever was used to predict who would achieve at a more rapid rate. Children were just picked at random.

The startling fact, however, was that most of these children did bloom—and that blooming could be measured even on IQ tests. Nearly four out of five first and second graders improved their IQ scores by 10 points in the course of that year. Almost half of the students improved by 20 IQ points, and more than one in five gained at least 30 IQ points. Students in the upper grades did not improve so dramatically, but their improvement was also significant in comparison to that of the students whose teachers were not told they would bloom.

Not all teacher expectancies are likely to produce such dramatic self-fulfilling prophecy effects. Some studies have found much smaller effects, and some have found none at all. This latter finding is encouraging, for it indicates that it is possible for teachers to prevent expectancies from having too large an impact. This is particularly important because so many expectancies come from unconscious biases. Gender, ethnic, and racially based expectancies have been demonstrated in a variety of studies, but other expectancies far exceed these in their routine impact in regular classrooms.

Almost anything about a student can establish an expectancy in the mind of a teacher, potentially leading to a self-fulfilling prophecy—the physical attractiveness of the student, the accent of the student, the cleanliness of the student, the amount of attention the student gives the teacher, the student's name, to whom the student is related, the promptness of the student, the kind of hairstyle the student wears, what the teacher who had the student last year says about the student, material in the student's personal record, the athletic ability of the student, the musical ability of the student, and on and on. All of these things have some impact—impact that may be either positive or negative but that has nothing to do with the student's real intellectual ability.

What kind of people were the teachers in the Pygmalion study and those that followed? No, they were not some special, defective breed of humans. They were just normal teachers, normal human beings. The behaviors observed in this research were much like those observed in a wide variety of other research studies. One of the major problems in medical research, for example, is the impact of expectancies. There is an amazing tendency for people who think they are going to get well to actually get well. Sometimes drugs are credited with saving a person's life, when in fact the drug was nothing more than a sugar pill. This kind of a pill is known as a "placebo," and such expectancy effects are called "placebo effects." In other cases, people have serious side effects, such as nausea and vertigo, from harmless medications because they believe the medications are likely to produce these effects. This is the reason the U.S. government has very high standards for the approval of new medications. If a human can make her- or himself sick or well as a function of expectancies, is it any wonder that a human teacher can get better (or worse) performance from a student as a function of expectancies?

Children are not only affected by communication from teachers who have certain expectancies about them. Everyone develops expectancies about people with whom they come in contact, and communicates in a manner consistent with those expectancies. For children, then, the expectancies of their siblings, their parents, their peers, and others in their community all affect the behavior of people with whom they communicate. Thus, we should recognize the limits of the potential impact of teacher expectancies. However, we should never lose sight of how positive or negative expectancies for students can be acquired through such everyday encounters as talking with other teachers in the teachers' lounge (if you are fortunate enough to have one) or the lunchroom.

Self-Esteem

Although teacher expectancies can have a very large and significant impact on students, the student's own expectancies are likely to have an even greater impact. One's expectancies about one's own ability and likelihood of success rest on the foundation of one's self-esteem. A person's self-esteem has a strong genetic base. As a consequence, it is very difficult to change after the formative years. Hence, it is vital that a child build as positive a self-esteem as is possible in the early grades. Later may be too late.

Self-esteem not only determines a student's expectancies, it also influences how the student interprets the outcome of her or his efforts. Figure 9.1 is intended to illustrate how this works. In the figure we have classified students as either high or low in self-esteem. Similarly, we have classified the outcome of the student's effort (as evaluated by an impartial outside observer) as either a success or a failure.

As indicated in Figure 9.1, students with high self-esteem attribute their successes to their ability and their failures to bad luck. Such attributions protect the high self-esteem of these students. Even if the student does very badly, it is not

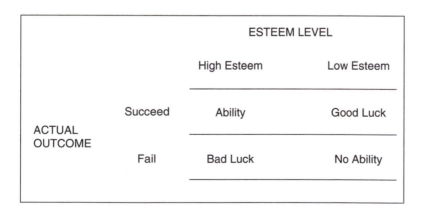

FIGURE 9.1   *Success/Failure Attributions and Self-Esteem*

seen as a function of lack of ability; it is just luck. In most cases, the student will continue to expect success in similar situations.

By contrast, students with low self-esteem attribute their failures to their lack of ability and their successes to good luck. Here, too, students' attributions will protect their self-esteem—in this case, low self-esteem. Even if the student does very well, it is seen not as a function of ability but simply as good luck. Thus, in most cases the student will continue to expect failure in similar situations.

The powerful impact of these expectations based on self-esteem is often very frustrating to teachers. No matter what the teacher says or does—even when the teacher goes to great lengths to demonstrate to the student that he or she has ability—the low-self-esteem student is unlikely to change her or his self-esteem. It is very important, then, that teachers in the early grades communicate a sense of self-worth to their students. Self-fulfilling prophecies do not have to be bad. If teachers can instill positive self-esteem in students in the early years, those positive self-fulfilling prophecies can continue though the rest of the students' lives.

It is important, however, that teachers do not take this advice too far. What is needed are *accurate* self-esteem perceptions, not perceptions that are too high or too low. Often, children are told that their abilities—particularly in such areas as music, sports, and the arts—are much greater than they actually are. This frequently leads to major disappointments later on, and can result in very poor attitudes toward other aspects of education. Students do not realize that, regardless of their abilities, they are more likely to be hit by lightning than to make it to the NBA or to Carnegie Hall! For a teacher to build false self-esteem does no child a favor. This behavior should be recognized as a particularly cruel form of child abuse.

Expectancies and Grouping

It is a simple fact that students must be placed into groups for purposes of instruction. Grouping students, however, has a heavy impact on the communication environment of the student, and hence that of the teacher. To understand how this impact is related to expectancies and teacher–student communication, we need to examine both the reasons for grouping and the types of groups commonly formed in schools.

Reasons for Grouping

There are at least three categories of reasons for grouping: administrative, sociological, and learning. Often, these are in conflict with one another, and sometimes one category completely dominates the other two.

1. *Administrative reasons.* Whenever there are more students than can be taught in one place by one teacher, the students must be divided into smaller groups of some type. The only real exception to this general rule that students always must be grouped is the one-room schoolhouse. Although this was a common context for teaching in the early history of this country—one that continues to the present in very sparsely populated areas—very few students today attend school in such an environment. And even in a one-room schoolhouse, not all students are taught together.

Because grouping by some characteristic or characteristics of the students may facilitate matching teachers' abilities and interests to those of students, it is often administratively advantageous to do so. Many different characteristics can be, and have been, employed by various administrative units. These include such characteristics as biological sex, racial or ethnic group, age level, achievement level, ability level, and student interest, among others. Obviously, some of these characteristics are no longer considered appropriate—or even legal—to use as a basis for grouping.

2. *Sociological reasons.* Throughout history, people with similar backgrounds have been drawn together by their common interests, beliefs, and attitudes. Thus, if given the choice, students will typically group themselves in this way. The principle of homophily, which we considered in Chapters 3 and 7, suggests that communication in such groups will be lively and effective, and the frequency of serious misunderstandings will be lower than in more diverse groups. It is not unreasonable to expect that learning could be facilitated by such grouping. However, if such groups are formed by someone other than the students themselves—for example, a teacher or administrator—they may today be considered illegal. Beyond that, many people believe that learning in tight, sociologically similar groups actually stifles important types of growth.

It is social policy in many areas to place students in highly diverse groups so they will have the opportunity to learn to communicate and live with people who are very different from themselves. Although some believe that such groupings facilitate the learning of sociologically important skills, others believe that such groups inhibit the learning of more traditional academic objectives. Whichever view prevails, the resulting group assignments reflect a sociological judgment. Thus, it is not so much whether one will employ sociological criteria in grouping as which criteria will be employed.

3. *Learning reasons.* Although the reasons for grouping just mentioned have clear implications for learning, that is not their primary focus. In this category, learning is advanced with a specific rationale. There are a number of different learning rationales, and hence grouping approaches, that have been advanced. We will look at just four as representative examples.

a. *Grouping by achievement level.* It is argued that students who are achieving at the same level make the best groups. They have close competition, all of the individuals know about as much as one another, the lessons can be carefully adapted to them without fear of leaving some students behind, and the students can communicate with one another on the same level. Some argue that this approach is particularly good for students who are high or low achievers, because both are likely to lose out in classes directed toward average students. Opponents of this approach, including some teachers, are concerned that placing students in low-achievement groups can damage their self-esteem and motivation, and that placing students in high-achievement groups may inflate their ego and make them intolerant of other students. They also argue that this kind of grouping does not allow students to learn to communicate well with people who are different from themselves.

b. *Grouping by ability level.* This type of grouping is very similar to the preceding one, but the rationale is slightly different. In the previous type, achievement test scores would likely be used to group the students. In this type, ability test scores would be employed instead. Thus, it is argued, students of nearly equal ability will challenge each other more and are likely to motivate those students who would not otherwise work up to their ability. The criticisms of this rationale are about the same as those for achievement grouping. However, the students may be more different in achievement from each other in this system, thus blunting to some extent the concern about students not learning to communicate with people different from themselves.

c. *Grouping by learning style.* Strong arguments are made that students do not all learn in the same ways. (For a more extensive discussion of learning style, see Richmond and Gorham, 1998.) Hence, if all students are taught in the same style, some will not learn as well as others. If visual learners, for example, are grouped together and taught using visual techniques, they will learn more than if they were taught with other techniques. The research on learning styles is extensive and clearly indicates that there are very large differences in learning styles among students. Since it is difficult, if not impossible, to adapt to all of these learning styles in a class of students with heterogeneous learning styles, it seems to follow that the best way to use the information from this research is as a basis for grouping. Critics of this approach say that it can be difficult to measure learning style or to find teachers who want to teach with a given style.

d. *Systematic grouping for differences.* All of the rationales for grouping discussed so far emphasize the desirability of putting students who are alike together so they will learn more. This rationale is virtually the opposite. It holds that students learn best when the variability in learners is greatest. In particular, this approach views peer teaching (students teaching other students) as especially valuable. Opponents of this view see it as overly idealistic. They suggest that peer teaching seldom occurs and that the teacher is run ragged trying to adapt everything to so many different types of students.

In sum, arguments for and against various types of grouping center on rationales that are drawn from administrative, sociological, or learning concerns or some combination thereof. Although we have referenced some different types of groups in this discussion, we now need to direct our attention specifically to the various types of groups so that we will be able to show how the varying rationales and types come together.

Types of Groupings

Although there are many, many different types of groupings, we will consider four of the most commonly employed here, and briefly mention a fifth that is the most common of all. The four types of groups we will consider first are universal ability, subject-matter ability, heterogeneous, and random.

1. *Universal ability.* Here we will use ability and achievement as if they were the same thing, although, as we have noted, they reference different types of measures for assignment to groups. This approach is very common. It makes it possible for teachers to specialize in working with high-, moderate-, or low-ability groups. Students of similar ability can be expected to progress at similar rates, although certainly not at identical ones. Communication between students is enhanced by their similarities. Instructional communication, similarly, is enhanced by decreasing the need for diverse adaptation on the part of the teacher.

This type of grouping is often criticized on political grounds because "advantaged" students tend to fall into certain groups and "disadvantaged" students into others. When this happens, it is increasingly likely that such groups will be stereotyped on ethnic or racial grounds. Even when all of the students are ethnically and racially similar, this type of grouping is criticized because it reduces the opportunities for peer teaching and increases the likelihood that students in higher-ability groups will develop feelings of superiority and those in lower-ability groups will have feelings of inferiority.

2. *Subject-matter ability.* This is similar to universal ability grouping except that students move from one group to another on the basis of their ability in a specific subject. Thus, theoretically at least, a student could be, for example, in the top group for math, a middle group for English, and a low group for art. The presumed advantages of this type of grouping are the same as those for universal ability grouping, as are the criticisms. However, this approach creates even more tightly matched groups, because few students are really good at everything or poor at everything. It is also believed that, because students move from group to group, problems related to self-esteem are reduced, as are ethnic/racial concerns.

3. *Heterogeneous.* Both universal and subject-matter grouping are examples of homogeneous grouping—that is, grouping together people who are alike in some way. Heterogeneous grouping is the opposite. It involves systematically placing students with very different abilities in the same group. This type of grouping is justified on the grounds of increasing opportunities for peer teaching and for students to learn to communicate with students very different from themselves. Heterogeneous grouping is often more politically acceptable to the various constituencies within a community than either of the first two types.

4. *Random.* Grouping students randomly is like placing students in a class by drawing their names out of a hat. For some, this is the preferred type of grouping because it will presumably provide diversity in each class (although that is not guaranteed as it is with heterogeneous grouping). The alleged advantages are essentially the same as those of heterogeneous grouping, but they are presumed to be achieved without consideration of ability or achievement scores in making group assignments. Although severe distortions in the distribution of students to groups is still possible under this method, random grouping has the major advantage that those problems are not produced by biased or capricious behavior on the part of those who make the assignments. Hence, this approach is often employed when there is conflict among various political factions in the community. It is the only grouping type that has no real learning advantage associated with it. When it is chosen, it is as a result of administrative and/or sociological reasons.

The final type of grouping really is a nontype: *chaotic.* Unfortunately, this is probably the most common way that groups are formed in many schools. Often there are so many forces pulling and tugging that no systematic type of grouping is possible at all. In a small high school, for example, classes may be grouped into the "band group" and "others" because the band practices during the school day and non–band members can take other classes during that period. Thus, there may be two English classes—the band group and the "other" group. Similarly, students are assigned to one English class or the other for a reason that has absolutely nothing to do with English at all.

Figure 9.2 presents the four main types of grouping in contrast with the three primary reasons for grouping. As you can see in that figure, each type of group may be used or rejected for more than one reason. Similarly, from whatever rationale base one approaches grouping, there is more than one type of grouping that may be chosen or rejected. It should be no surprise, then, that there are many conflicts in school systems over grouping.

You may have noticed by now that we have not included communication as a fourth category of reasons for grouping. We did not do so because communication is

	REASONS FOR GROUPING		
Types of Groups	*Administrative*	*Sociological*	*Learning*
Universal ability	X		X
Subject ability	X		X
Heterogeneous		X	X
Random	X	X	

FIGURE 9.2 *Types of Groups and Reasons for Grouping*

seldom a reason used to make such decisions. From an instructional-communication vantage point, however, it is hard to argue against some form of ability grouping. It requires enormous ability and effort for a teacher to adapt her or his communication to an extremely diverse group of students; what normally happens in such circumstances is that instruction is directed toward the middle, and the stronger and weaker students are more or less left to fend for themselves.

The biggest problem with grouping is in the expectancies that are produced by whatever type of grouping is employed. If some form of homogeneous grouping is used, some consistency in behavior is expected from students in each group. Heterogeneous grouping, on the other hand, creates the expectancy that some of the students will do well and others will fail. This is the assumption under the "normal curve" that is used in many educational settings.

Major questions always arise concerning grouping. Is it best for students who are alike to be able to be grouped together? Is it necessary for students who are "different" to be mainstreamed? Can "disadvantaged" students best be helped by participating in homogeneous groups or in diverse groups? No matter how these questions are answered, expectancies for students are established. Some are positive, and some are negative. It is important that the teacher be able to identify both kinds of expectancies and strive to keep the negative ones, at least, from influencing the way the teacher communicates with the student.

References

Richmond, V. P., & Gorham, J. S. (1998). *Communication, learning, and affect in instruction.* Acton, MA: Tapestry Press.

Rosenthal, R., & Jacobson, L. (1968). *Pygmalion in the classroom.* New York: Holt.

Glossary

expectancies   Predictions of future occurrences.

heterogeneous grouping   The assignment of students to groups because they are different from one another in terms of selected characteristics.

homogeneous grouping   The assignment of students to groups because they are similar to one another in terms of selected characteristics.

self-esteem   An individual's evaluation of her or his own worth.

self-fulfilling prophecies   A prediction that comes true in part because one expects it to come true.

10

Willingness to Communicate

People differ greatly in the degree to which they communicate. At the extremes, some students hardly ever speak, while others seem to talk continually. Teachers, too, vary widely in terms of how much they talk. Some seem to be talking to their classes all day long, while others seem to talk very seldom.

This variability in talking behavior has been the object of study by scholars in several disciplines for decades. In fact, research in this area represents one of the longest continuous streams of research in the social sciences. In recent years, three distinct branches of this research have formed. One of these is concerned with "communication apprehension" (McCroskey, 1984)—the fear or anxiety associated with communication, a topic we will consider in some detail in Chapter 11. The other two branches, "shyness" and "willingness to communicate," will be considered in this chapter.

"Shyness," as we will consider that term here, refers to the actual talking frequency of an individual (McCroskey & Richmond, 1982). That is, a person who refrains from talking much of the time can be referred to as a "shy" individual. Simply put, in this context, shyness is the behavior of not talking, whatever the reason or reasons the person has for that behavior.

"Willingness to communicate" refers to an individual's preference for initiating or avoiding communication (McCroskey, 1992; McCroskey & Richmond, 1987). That is, a person who prefers to initiate communication in many circumstances is referred to as "highly willing to communicate." By contrast, a person who prefers to avoid communication in many circumstances is seen as "not willing to communicate." "Willingness to communicate," then, refers to a person's preferences with regard to initiating or avoiding communication, while "shyness" refers to a person's actual behavior with regard to initiating or avoiding communication.

Although it would be expected that in most situations a person will behave in the way he or she prefers to behave, it should be recognized that many other factors, in addition to behavioral preferences, may influence people's actual behavioral choices. As a simple example, we might prefer to pick up an unattended $20 bill on a counter, but our moral values or fear of being caught is likely to prevent us from engaging in our preferred behavior.

The Willingness-to-Communicate Trait

Consistent behavioral tendencies with regard to an individual's frequency and amount of talk have been noted in the social science literature for decades. Such regularity in communication behavior across communication contexts suggests the presence of a traitlike personality variable. This willingness-to-communicate trait drives an individual's behavior across contexts and explains why people with different levels of this trait can be observed engaging in differing behavioral patterns (McCroskey, 1992).

Early research by Cattell (1973) and Buss and Plomin (1975) strongly suggested that this trait is biologically heritable. More recent research has confirmed a strong link between genetics and both temperament and some communication traits, such as shyness and willingness to communicate (Eysenck, 1990; McCroskey, Heisel, & Richmond, 2001). Shyness is negatively associated with extraversion and positively associated with neuroticism. Willingness to communicate is positively associated with extraversion and negatively associated with neuroticism. However, willingness to communicate and shyness are also influenced by a person's communication experiences and the culture in which he or she lives. Thus, an individual's talking behavior is relatively consistent across contexts, but not perfectly consistent. That is, if a student is seen talking a lot in class, it is likely that the student will be seen talking a lot on the playground as well. However, a student who talks a lot with friends may not be willing to communicate in the classroom as a function of her or his previous experiences with the classroom. Thus, even though all people have a trait level of willingness to communicate, which may range from very low to very high, they do not necessarily exhibit that trait equally in all types of communication contexts or with all type of receivers.

Types of Contexts

Although there are many types of communication context, we will look at four types here as examples that are particularly relevant to the classroom: dyadic, small-group, large-group, and public.

1. *Dyadic communication.* Dyadic communication involves two people and includes what we normally call "conversation." When one student talks to another, or a student talks to a teacher, we have dyadic communication. The overwhelming majority of the communication in which most people engage is dyadic communication. It is the least threatening type of communication for most (but definitely not all) people, and it is the type of context in which most people are most willing to communicate.

2. *Small-group communication.* Small-group communication involves more people than dyadic communication, but the upper limit of people to be considered a small group is a matter of judgment. At some point, probably around 10 or 12 people but in some cases as high as 15, people no longer see themselves as being in such a group. In classrooms, small groups usually include about 4 to 7 people. Breaking into such groups provides more opportunities for students to talk about a given topic than would exist in a general class discussion. People vary greatly in their response to communication opportunities in small groups; some are highly talkative, while others choose to say virtually nothing unless pushed into doing so by other group members.

3. *Large-group communication.* Large-group communication is represented by the typical classroom context. In this context, someone is directing the interaction of the other people in the group. In the classroom, it usually is the teacher; in other meetings it may be a chair of the group. The willingness to communicate of most people drops sharply in large groups. Unless special efforts are made to encourage, or virtually force, people to participate, most people will not talk at all. A few very verbal people are likely to dominate the interaction in such contexts. This is particularly true in classrooms. Observations of classrooms indicate that 10 percent of the students typically account for 70 percent of the talk. Requiring classroom participation changes this proportion only slightly, but it does make students who are not willing to communicate in such contexts very uncomfortable, and, as we will note later, may substantially reduce the amount the students learn in the class.

4. *Public communication.* Public communication involves one person speaking before a group of other people. This public-speaking context is the most threatening communication context for most people. Very few individuals are highly willing to communicate in this context. Many people will do almost anything to avoid giving a public speech. However, many classroom experiences involve public speaking. Such common assignments as show-and-tell, oral reading, oral current events, oral book reports, and science projects are examples of public communication that may happen in a classroom. When given free choice, many students will simply drop classes that require such communication. Others will stay home "sick" on days when such assignments are required. It is important for individual teachers to recognize that many classes, not just public-speaking classes, require students to give public speeches. And students who hate public-speaking classes are likely to hate these other classes just as much.

In general, the more people who are likely to hear one speak, the more threatening the context is seen to be. Thus, in general, the more people in the "audience," the less willing to communicate a person will be. Of course, threat can be a function of something other than number of people. For example, a job interview usually involves only the interviewer and the interviewee, a dyadic context, or perhaps just the interviewee and a few other people, a small-group context. Nevertheless, job interviews are highly threatening to most people.

Types of Receivers

Although there are many types of receivers, we will consider three types here as examples: strangers, acquaintances, and friends. In many instances in the classroom, people begin as strangers, become acquaintances, and may then become friends.

Most people are least willing to communicate with strangers and most willing to communicate with friends. Acquaintances fall in between these extremes. Although generally people are least willing to communicate with strangers, much everyday communication does involve such interactions. Whenever we shop, we are likely to be served by strangers, unless we live in a very small community. Similarly, whenever we travel, most of our contacts are with strangers.

In the instructional environment, most classes in higher education begin with the class members being strangers or, at best, acquaintances. The same thing is true in large high schools. At the elementary level, except for the first year a student attends the school, many of the children are at least acquainted, and some are friends. In some instances, virtually an entire class of fourth graders may have been together as third graders the previous year.

Students, like others, find uncertainty in communication discomforting. Hence, when confronted with people they do not know well, they recognize that one way to avoid such discomfort is to refrain from communication as much as possible. This applies to students' reactions to teachers as well as their reactions to one another. Often, therefore, teachers will find it easier to get better acquainted with a given student if they wait a while to initiate dyadic interactions. As the student becomes more familiar with the teacher, he or she may become more willing to interact with the teacher on that level.

It is important to recognize that both context type and receiver type have simultaneous impact on individuals' willingness to communicate. Thus, although the prospect of having a dyadic interaction with a friend may find the person highly willing to communicate, the prospect of dyadic interaction with a stranger may generate a very different response. Similarly, the prospect of giving a speech before a group of friends may be seen as an unpleasant but tolerable task, but the prospect of giving a speech before a group of strangers may be seen as a completely unacceptable one. Even though willingness to communicate is an individual trait, then, few people are equally willing to communicate in all contexts with all people. Both context type and receiver type make a difference.

Special Constraints

As we have indicated, people have a willingness-to-communicate trait that, in general, can predict how much they want to communicate in various contexts and with various people. Although trait willingness to communicate is very strong, people will vary to some extent in the degree to which they actually communicate even in highly similar contexts and/or with highly similar types of receivers. Situations make different demands, so behavior may be different, even though the person's level of trait willingness to communicate stays the same. Both situational constraints and personal constraints can influence a student's willingness to communicate in the classroom.

Situational Constraints

There are numerous situational factors that may call for differences in students' willingness to communicate in the classroom. Something as simple as the temperature of the room can have a noticeable impact. When the room is too warm (above 72 degrees), the teacher may notice a significant drop in total participation in classroom interaction. Warmth tends to slow down intellectual processes and make students drowsy. When that happens, willingness to communicate will decrease.

Teachers often reduce students' willingness to communicate by not appearing open to student communication or by being highly evaluative of what students say. If students think talk is not acceptable or desirable, or if they feel they are likely to be criticized for what they say, most of them are bright enough to stay silent. It is not that they are less willing to communicate in all classrooms, just that they are not willing to communicate in this particular one.

In some situations, students put high pressure on one another not to communicate in the classroom. Although this may be a general orientation, it is more likely to be related to something specific—for example, when it is shortly before the time for the class to end. The student may still want to participate but may recognize that the other students will punish her or him for doing so.

Students' willingness to communicate may also be reduced because of affective concerns. It the student does not like the subject matter or does not like the teacher, her or his willingness to communicate is likely to be sharply reduced.

These are just a few of the situational constraints that may exist. Others include such factors as an upcoming holiday, a student activity or ball game later in the day, the presence of the principal or some other visitor sitting in the room, and so on. The teacher may have no way of knowing why a student is quiet on a given day; even the student may not know why. The best advice for the teacher is to simply recognize that the student does not want to talk and to leave her or him alone. Even if the student knows why he or she does not want to talk, the reason may be something he or she does not want to share with the teacher. Often, it is a personal rather than a situational constraint.

Personal Constraints

There are an unlimited number of personal constraints that may influence a student's willingness to communicate in the classroom. The one that teachers usually suspect first may actually be the correct one: The student has not prepared well enough for class. This, however, is not as common as most teachers think. Sometimes a student is fully prepared but just doesn't have anything to say.

A student's health may have a big impact on her or his willingness to communicate. When one is not feeling well, it is reasonable to want to refrain from communicating. Sometimes the student is just feeling tired and having a hard time following what is going on.

More serious student concerns can also be present. Sometimes teachers ask questions of a class that a student feels call for self-disclosure, which he or she is unwilling to provide. Sometimes, a student is having personal or family problems and simply does not want to share those with the rest of the students.

As we indicated with situational constraints, the teacher who recognizes that a student wants to remain silent should leave the student alone. Students are people, and people have the right to be quiet if they want to. Although quietness has a price for the student, it is not the right of the teacher to force the student to communicate. The mere fact that a person is a teacher does not mean that he or she is entitled to breach a student's desire for privacy. To coerce the student to communicate against her or his will can only damage the relationship between the teacher and that student and thereby reduce student learning.

Correlates of Willingness to Communicate

Although it appears that the willingness-to-communicate trait is produced by an interaction of genetic and learning factors, there are a number of other factors that are also theoretically related to willingness to communicate and that may help us to understand this trait better. Research studies (McCroskey & McCroskey, 1986a, 1986b) have found that each of these individual difference variables correlates either positively or negatively with willingness to communicate. We will consider each of these in turn: extraversion, anomie and alienation, self-esteem, cultural diversity and divergence, communication competence, and communication apprehension.

Extraversion

Extraversion has been studied as a personality variable for decades. The construct posits a continuum between extreme extraversion and extreme introversion. The nearer the individual is to the extraversion extreme, the more "people-oriented" the person is likely to be. Extraverts tend be sociable and have a high need for interaction with other people. They need to be linked to others and may quickly develop feelings of loneliness in the absence of others. The more extraverted the person, the more willing to communicate he or she is likely to be. The extraverted student will like to work with groups and may be a classroom leader.

The more introverted the individual, the less need he or she will feel for communication and the less value he or she will place on communicating. Introverts tend to be inner-directed and introspective. They also tend to be less sociable and less dependent on others' evaluations than more extraverted people. The introvert prefers the pleasure of her or his own company. The more introverted the person, the less willing to communicate he or she is likely to be. The introverted student usually will prefer to work and study alone; he or she often will strongly dislike working in groups and may even refuse to do so.

Anomie and Alienation

Anomie and alienation are not exactly the same thing, but they are close enough to consider together. Anomie refers to a state in which an individual's normative standards are severely reduced or lost. The anomic person is essentially "norm-less." Such people do not internalize society's norms or values, including the value of communication. Alienation is an extreme manifestation of anomie. Alienated people feel estranged from the surrounding society. They consider themselves to be apart from and unrelated to other people and society as a whole.

Both of these orientations have been found to be associated with negative attitudes toward communication. In addition, the behavior patterns of people with these orientations are likely to be highly similar to those of people with a very low willingness to communicate. Although students of any age may be anomic or alienated, extreme manifestations of these orientations are sometimes seen in students who are heavily involved with drugs or who are simply staying in school until the age when the law will permit them to quit. It is unlikely that teachers will be able to draw such students into classroom interaction, even under the best of conditions. Hence, in the absence of interventions designed specifically for these students, the teacher is wise to let them remain quiet.

Self-Esteem

Self-esteem refers to a person's evaluation of her or his own worth. Research has determined that self-esteem has a strong genetic base. Therefore, teachers' attempts to change a student's self-esteem are not likely to be successful. A student who has low self-esteem may be expected to be less willing to communicate because of a feeling that he or she has little of value to say. These students also are likely to believe that others will respond negatively to whatever they might say; to avoid such negative responses, they may refrain from communicating when possible. As noted in Chapter 9, self-esteem has a profound impact on the way students see others' behavior in relation to themselves. Thus, teachers are unlikely to get students with low self-esteem to change their reluctance to communicate. Whatever the teacher says or does will be interpreted through that self-esteem screen and will likely be discounted.

Cultural Diversity and Divergence

Among other things, cultural diversity refers to differences between cultures in terms of how each culture values and rewards communication. People in some cultures report a substantially lower average willingness to communicate than those in some other cultures (McCroskey & Richmond, 1990). Thus, in a multicultural classroom, it should be expected that observed differences in willingness to communicate will be in part a function of the different cultures that make up the students' backgrounds.

When students from other countries are present in a classroom, the teacher should make considerable effort to determine the value placed on communication and the communication norms in the foreign culture and to adapt to those values and norms when interacting with the foreign student. Because all students assume that the values present in their native culture are the correct values, such issues need to be dealt with very carefully.

Cultural divergence refers to the degree to which one student's cultural background differs from that of the other students in the classroom. We are not so much concerned here with differences in norms and values as they relate directly to communication. Rather, our concern is with the broad range of differences between the cultures in terms of human behavior and attitudes in general.

When a student is a member of a minority in a classroom, especially a very small minority, that fact usually has a strong depressing effect on the individual's willingness to communicate. Even for those who are highly willing to communicate in other environments in which they are members of the majority culture, their orientation is likely to change when they move into an environment in which they are in the minority. As minority students become more familiar with the norms of the majority culture, they are likely to be able to adapt to them and become more willing to communicate. This can be facilitated by the support and encouragement of the teacher. If students from two cultures are hostile to each other, however, this adaptation is unlikely to occur.

Communication Competence

If one person does not know the language others are using, it is a virtual certainty that that person will not be willing to communicate. What is true of language competence is true of communication competence in general.

The key here, however, is not so much the actual communication competence of the individual as it is the individual's self-perceived communication competence. People do not always make decisions about whether or not to be willing to communicate on the basis of their actual competence. Rather, they make such decisions on the basis of their self-perception of their own competence. It is quite possible for a person to be woefully incompetent and still be willing to communicate —we hear them just about every day. Similarly, it is possible for a person to be quite competent but not self-perceive her- or himself in that way. This may be a function of low self-esteem, or it may just be a distorted perception. In any event, self-perceived communication competence is highly associated with willingness to communicate, particularly in the general U.S. culture.

Communication Apprehension

The most heavily researched area related to willingness to communicate is communication apprehension. This is *an individual's level of fear or anxiety associated with either real or anticipated communication with another person or persons.* The higher a person's communication apprehension, the lower her or his willingness to communicate will be. Since this is the topic for Chapter 11, we will not consider it more thoroughly here.

Effects of Low Willingness to Communicate

Since the title of this section may be somewhat misleading, let us clarify what we are considering here. The only direct effect presumed to be produced by a person's low level of willingness to communicate is a reduction in the amount that person talks. Thus, we might better title this section "the effects of shy behavior" or "the effects of not talking." In any event, the effects of being quiet rather than talkative have been the target of hundreds of research studies. We now have a very clear picture of these effects, and they are overwhelmingly negative, at least in the general U.S. culture. We will summarize the effects in three categories that relate to three environments for communication: the work environment, the social environment, and, most important for our concerns here, the instructional environment. For more expanded summaries of this research, you may wish to read the chapters by Richmond (1984) and by Daly and Stafford (1984) and/or the short book specifically directed toward the classroom problems in this area (McCroskey & Richmond, 1991).

Work Environment

In earlier times, much of society's work was performed by individuals, often working alone. In contemporary society, however, much work must be done in groups, often in very large, complex organizations. Communication among workers is critical, and its absence may result in complete failure. It should not be surprising to learn, then, that an individual's willingness to communicate can have a significant impact on her or his success in the contemporary workplace.

The effect can begin long before a person is even hired. A letter of recommendation that notes in passing that a job applicant is quiet is likely to reduce the applicant's chances of even getting an interview for the job. Even if the person is chosen for an interview, his or her quietness is likely to result in a negative evaluation and, hence, not being hired.

If the person is hired, it is likely that the position will be a lower-paying one, since higher-paying positions regularly require a lot of communication. Once the person is hired, personnel reviews will probably be lower, indicating the individual is less competent in her or his work. Such reviews are consistent with the views of peers in the workplace, who are likely to rule out a quiet person as an opinion leader in the work group. The quiet person is more likely to be selected for layoffs or terminations. Certainly not surprisingly, the person is less likely to be promoted in the organization. In fact, research has indicated that many quiet people actually do not want to be promoted because they recognize that the communication demands are much greater in higher positions.

Clearly, the stereotypes associated with the conceptions that "communication is a good thing" and "the more communication the better" appear to be alive and well in organizational society. But before we castigate hiring and firing officers in our organizations too much, we might want to explore whether their decisions actually make good corporate sense.

What might we be told if we asked our employment officer about these decisions? We might learn that employees who don't ask questions make more mistakes. Mistakes cost the company money. In most organizations, virtually all positions above the lowest entry level are supervisory positions. Success in such positions depends on high-quality communication skills. For the company to get the most out of an employee, that person must communicate ideas and suggestions. An employee who won't talk is depriving the organization of her or his expertise.

Simply put, then, organizations have very good reasons for rejecting people who appear to be unwilling to communicate. Their rejection is not simply based on stereotypes and misconceptions. For many jobs, quiet employees are indeed inferior to employees who are willing to communicate.

Social Environment

To have a social relationship, a person must communicate. Not communicating with another person effectively indicates a lack of concern for them. It says, "I do not like you" loudly and clearly.

Research involving quietness in the social arena presents a picture very much like that in the work environment. People who are not willing to communicate are seen as less attractive and credible by others around them. Few people know them well enough even to classify them as acquaintances. They have fewer friends than other people, in some cases none at all. They are likely to consider themselves to be lonely people. During high school, college, and young adulthood, they have fewer dates—less than half as many, on average, as people do who are more willing to communicate. Some have no dates at all. If they date, they tend to date one person only and are likely to marry that person at a younger age than their peers who are more willing to communicate.

The social picture of the person who is not willing to communicate is not a pretty one. It is an image of a lonely person with few social contacts. Again, as in the work environment, this social rejection does not come from some sinister source. It is the natural outgrowth of not being willing to communicate. When two people meet, they are hesitant to interact with each other because each has a high degree of uncertainty about how the other person will respond to her or him. Communication, even at a trivial level, is what allows them to begin to reduce that uncertainty and become comfortable with each other. A person who is not willing to communicate causes the uncertainty level to remain high and, in effect, drives the other person away.

School Environment

Based on how people who are not willing to communicate are treated in the work and social environments, it should be no surprise that students who are not willing to communicate often do not fare well in school. Such students seldom, if ever, participate in class discussions or seek out the teacher outside of class to clarify ideas in the course. They are seen by teachers as less intelligent than students who are more willing to communicate, and expectations for their success are low. As might be expected, quiet students are likely to be members of few if any student activity groups. Students who are not willing to communicate actually do learn less, dislike school more, and are more likely to drop out.

As we noted earlier in this book, the educational system in the United States tends to emphasize communication as a means of learning. As a result, students who are less willing to communicate actually learn less and find the learning environment more punishing and less rewarding than do other students.

On balance, then, being willing to communicate is a very positive attribute in contemporary society. Children who are not willing to communicate grow up to be adults who are not willing to communicate and, in the process, often experience far fewer of life's benefits. Dealing with quiet children is one of the greatest challenges faced by teachers. We will consider several things teachers can do to help quiet children—or at least to avoid making things worse for them—in Chapter 11, after we first consider one of the major factors that causes children and adults to be unwilling to communicate—communication apprehension.

References

Buss, A. H., & Plomin, R. (1975). *A temperament theory of personality development.* New York: Wiley.

Cattell, R. B. (1973). *Personality and mood by questionnaire.* San Francisco: Jossey-Bass.

Daly, J. A., & Stafford, L. (1984). Correlates and consequences of social-communicative anxiety. In J. A. Daly & J. C. McCroskey (Eds.), *Avoiding communication: Shyness, reticence, and communication apprehension* (pp. 125–143). Beverly Hills, CA: Sage.

Eysenck, H. J. (1990). Biological dimensions of personality. In L. A. Pervin (Ed.), *Handbook of personality: Theory and research* (pp. 244–276). New York: Guilford.

McCroskey, J. C. (1984). The communication apprehension perspective. In J. A. Daly & J. C. McCroskey (Eds.), *Avoiding communication: Shyness, reticence, and communication apprehension* (pp. 13–38). Beverly Hills, CA: Sage.

McCroskey, J. C. (1992). Reliability and validity of the willingness to communicate scale. *Communication Quarterly, 40,* 16–25.

McCroskey, J. C., Heisel, A. D., & Richmond, V. P. (2001). Eysenck's BIG THREE and communication traits: Three correlational studies. *Communication Monographs, 68,* 360–366.

McCroskey, J. C., & McCroskey, L. L. (1986a, February). *Correlates of willingness to communicate.* Paper presented at the Western Speech Communication Association convention, Tucson, AZ.

McCroskey, J. C., & McCroskey, L. L. (1986b, November). *Communication competence and willingness to communicate.* Paper presented at the Speech Communication Association convention, Chicago.

McCroskey, J. C., & Richmond, V. P. (1982). Communication apprehension and shyness: Conceptual and operational distinctions. *Central States Speech Journal, 33,* 458–468.

McCroskey, J. C., & Richmond, V. P. (1987). Willingness to communicate. In J. C. McCroskey & J. A. Daly (Eds.), *Personality and interpersonal communication* (pp. 129–156). Newbury Park, CA: Sage.

McCroskey, J. C., & Richmond, V. P. (1990). Willingness to communicate: Differing cultural perspectives. *Southern Communication Journal, 56,* 72–77.

McCroskey, J. C., & Richmond, V. P. (1991). *Quiet children and the classroom teacher,* 2nd ed. Bloomington, IN: ERIC Clearinghouse on Reading and Communication Skills, and Annandale, VA: Speech Communication Association.

Richmond, V. P. (1984). Implications of quietness: Some facts and speculations. In J. A. Daly & J. C. McCroskey (Eds.), *Avoiding communication: Shyness, reticence, and communication apprehension* (pp. 145–155). Beverly Hills, CA: Sage.

Glossary

anomie and alienation   The tendency of some people not to adhere to the norms of the culture in which they live. It may involve estrangement from others and severely reduced communication with others.

communication apprehension   The fear or anxiety associated with either real or anticipated communication with another person or persons.

dyadic communication   Communication involving two people.

extraversion   A genetically based component of temperament. People who are high on the extraversion dimension of temperament tend to be outgoing, sociable, people-oriented, and communicative. People who are low on the extraversion dimension of temperament (introverts) tend to be the opposite.

self-perceived communication competence   An individual's evaluation of her or his own communication ability.

shyness   The behavior of not talking.

willingness to communicate   An individual's preference to initiate or avoid communication.

11

Communication Apprehension and Other Personality Traits

lauren

When we get to know someone, we are able to describe some unique characteristics of that individual and make some reliable predictions about how he or she will behave in various situations. We come to believe that, at least to some degree, we understand the person and how he or she is different from other people. We are then able to communicate with the person at what, in Chapter 3, we called the "psychological level."

Whether or not one has ever heard of the psychological level, as we have called it, it is likely most people will seek to communicate with others at that level, which is where communication is most effective and most comfortable. A major branch of the field of psychology is personality psychology. It is this branch that is most concerned with the study of how people systematically differ from one another.

The Nature of Personality

DW

Although most of us do not have the observational skills of the trained personality psychologist, we do function as amateur psychologists in our everyday lives. We seek to understand the personalities of the people around us. A person's personality is *the sum total of that individual's characteristics that make her or him unique.* Behavior is a reflection of personality; hence, we infer a person's personality by noting the way he or she behaves in various situations over a period of time. Based on such observations, we describe students with terms like quiet, manipulative, bullheaded, understanding, disagreeable, easy to get along with, defensive, egotistical, and so on.

Communication is a complex series of behaviors. Therefore, it is heavily influenced by personality (McCroskey & Daly, 1987). People with different kinds of personalities are likely to communicate in very different ways. It is important that we understand not only the personalities of our students but also our own personality. The way each of us communicates is in large measure a function of our own personality. Although it is easy for most of us to recognize that others have personalities, we are often among the last to recognize our own personality.

Personality drives behavior. Thus, a personality variable is a trait of an individual—that is, a regular part of the way that individual thinks, feels, and behaves. Traits can be changed, but only with considerable effort. A person who is bullheaded today most likely will still be bullheaded next year. Students usually are not particularly interested in changing their own personalities. Even if they are, they may not be able to do so without professional assistance. *We must plan to deal with students as they are, not as we would like them to be.*

When we say that personality drives behavior, we do not intend to suggest that behavior is never affected by the contexts in which one finds oneself. Actually, behavior is likely to be influenced by both context and personality most of the time. People tend to have some difficulty coping with that reality. When people are asked to explain human behaviors, it has been found they are likely to make what is called the "basic attribution error." That is, when explaining our students' bad behavior, we attribute the cause to personality, but when explaining our own bad behavior, we attribute it to the situation. The other person has an accident because he or she "is a careless driver"; we have an accident because "the visibility at that intersection was terrible." The student failed the test because he or she "is a goof-off who is too lazy to study"; we failed the test because "family commitments" prevented us from having the time to study. The opposite is also true: When explaining our students' good behavior, we attribute the cause to the context, but when explaining our own good behavior, we attribute it to our personality. Other people got home safely because they drove on good roads. We got home safely because we are careful drivers. The student did well on the test because it was an easy test. We got the tests graded on time because we are diligent teachers.

It is important that we become sensitive to this error. The student may be behaving in a particular way when around us but not when around other people. What we do or say may be creating a context that produces the observed behavior, which may not be characteristic of the student at all. In fact, what is happening may be a function of our own personality-driven behavior rather than the student's. Sometimes this point is brought home to teachers when they find that students are behaving differently in their class than in the classes of other teachers. Even then, however, some teachers do not consider the possibility that their own personality-driven behavior may be an important factor.

Common Personality Variables

There are a number of common personality variables that have an impact on the communication that is likely to occur in our classroom. We will consider a few of these as examples before turning our attention to the variable that may cause the most serious problems for many teachers and students.

Willingness to Communicate

As we noted in the previous chapter, students vary widely in their willingness to talk to others. This kind of personality orientation is manifested daily in most classrooms. We have already noted the problems faced by students who are quiet, and we will consider those problems in more detail later in this chapter. At this point, however, we want to look at the students at the opposite end of the continuum—those students who talk a lot.

When asked, almost every teacher can identify one or more of their students who they feel "talk too much." Interestingly, research indicates it is rare to find someone, student or otherwise, who actually talks too much, even though we all know someone who we think does so. The research indicates that the perception of talking too much is based on *what* the person says, not how much. In fact, when the content of what is said is held constant, research indicates that people are perceived more positively the more they talk, up to an extremely high level, a level beyond which almost no one goes!

Observations of regular classrooms indicate that teachers punish students for talking more than for any other behavior and that in many classrooms talking is punished more than all other behaviors combined. Although teachers may see the punishment as being for "disrupting class," students see it as being for talking, pure and simple. Even so, students whose personalities lead them to be highly willing to communicate do not usually reduce their talking behavior as a result of being punished for it. Students who are less willing to communicate, however, are likely to become even quieter as a result of such punishment in the classroom, even though the punishment is directed toward someone else rather than themselves. When teachers consistently punish high talkers, after a while, only the high talkers talk! Such is the nature of personality-driven behavior.

General Anxiety

If you observe almost any classroom, you will see the fidgeters, the nail-biters, and the cowering mice—the students who always seem to have a terrified look on their faces. These behaviors are manifestations of a personality orientation called general anxiety. Students with high general anxiety are, or at least seem to be, afraid of everything. Whether it be going out for recess, taking a test, answering a question, or simply starting a new unit, these students are fearful.

If the teacher is insensitive to this aspect of the student's personality, serious harm can be done. This orientation may be deeply rooted in the student's past experiences, experiences he or she may not even be able to remember. If there is a school psychologist, such students should be referred to that person. Teachers must be very careful not to make the student's problems worse. Forcing a person to engage in behaviors that are terrifying can have serious, long-lasting traumatic impact. All of us fear something—snakes, insects, heights, public speaking, roller coasters, water, public exposure—and may be able to visualize what it would be like for someone to force us to confront that particular thing. Students with high general anxiety may well fear all of these things, and many more. Although trained professionals sometimes use confrontation to help people overcome such fears, teachers do not have the legally required education and experience to know how to do this without exposing the student to major harm. Even if you are insensitive to what harm could come to the student, you need to be aware that engaging in such behavior may open you to serious, expensive legal problems.

Self-Concept and Self-Esteem

These two aspects of an individual's personality are often confused with each other. *Self-concept is the way a person sees herself or himself*—tall, athletic, outgoing, helpful, a fifth grader, a girl, and so on. It is how a person would describe her- or himself if asked to do so. *Self-esteem is the evaluation we place on ourselves*—good, useful, attractive, smart, or the opposite of any of these.

Students with low self-esteem feel they can't achieve much. They often have high general anxiety. They tend to blame themselves for all of their problems, even if by every objective standard they are blameless. They may be reluctant to participate in class because they think they have too little to offer. Students with high self-esteem, on the other hand, are very confident of their own abilities. They tend to blame others for any problems that they might have, and they sometimes become troublemakers in the classroom. They are likely to participate heavily in class, even if they don't have much to contribute. It is important that teachers realize that self-esteem has a strong genetic base. As a result, it is extremely hard, often impossible, to change people's self-esteem. It is best for teachers simply to accept students' varying levels of self-esteem and do their best to help all students no matter how those students see themselves.

Machiavellianism

This personality variable is named for Niccolò Machiavelli , the fifteenth-century author of *The Prince,* a classic manual for people who desired to be rulers. *The Prince* was most noted for its lack of moral concern and its advice on manipulation. One suggestion, for example, was directed toward the Prince who wanted to become a King: "First, kill all the other Princes."

High "Machs," as they are known, are manipulators. Low Machs are the people who get manipulated. From the earliest level of formal instruction, even in preschool, the full range of Machiavellianism is present in most classrooms. High Machs often have good communication and social skills. They are often able to develop positive relationships with their teachers. As a result, they may get away with all kinds of mischief in school. Low Machs often lack communication and social skills and sometimes become alienated from their teachers. They are the ones most likely to be caught and punished if they do something inappropriate at school.

The problem comes in when the high Mach does not have high moral standards, as is sometimes the case. High Machs are likely to be student leaders and also leaders of the drug pushers—sometimes both at the same time. These people grow up to be our political and religious leaders, the titans of industry, teachers and principals, union organizers, embezzlers, stock manipulators, and gang leaders. In school, they are unlikely to get in trouble, but the low Machs, the followers whom they have manipulated, may get into serious trouble.

Locus of Control

Locus of control has to do with where the individual sees the power over her or his life as residing. People with an internal locus of control see themselves as the masters of their own destiny. People with an external locus of control see themselves as pawns being manipulated by others. Whereas externals believe in chance or luck—"whatever will be, will be"—internals believe that only by their own hard work will they get ahead and succeed.

Internals often glory in their successes but are crushed by their failures. By contrast, externals are pleasantly surprised by their successes and relatively unperturbed by their failures. Teachers, even if they are externals themselves, often push students to be internals. The internalist values of individual responsibility and hard work are common themes in educational environments. Communication based on such values, of course, falls on the deaf ears of externally oriented students. These students are more likely to be moved by appeals indicating that a given behavior or group of behaviors will increase their chances of success.

Self-Awareness

Some people are very aware of their own being and of how they work. They figuratively turn their eyes inward and seek to see themselves as they really are. These people are referred to as privately self-aware. They would be self-aware even if isolated on a desert island. Other people are primarily aware of themselves as others see them. Their self-awareness is their image in the eyes of the people around them. They are publicly self-aware: They have no awareness of self apart from others.

People who are privately self-aware have little concern for projecting an image to others. Thus, their personalities may be obscured. To the extent, however, that one is able to perceive aspects of such an individual's personality, it is likely that those perceptions will be accurate. Because privately self-aware people are insensitive to how they are seen by others, they take no special pains to project a false impression. The publicly self-aware, on the other hand, live in the eyes of others. Hence, they actively try through their communication behaviors to project a personality they see as desirable.

Publicly aware students may take great pains to make the teacher see the positive aspects of their personalities while attempting to hide those they think are negative. We may be surprised, for example, when we learn that one of these students has cheated, because that was not an aspect of her or his personality that we had seen before. Privately aware students, on the other hand, are less well known but are likely to be seen more nearly as they really are, warts and all.

7 *Dogmatism*   *SF*

Dogmatism refers to the level of rigidity of a person's belief system. High "dogs" have very rigid belief systems; we might describe them as bullheaded or as "true believers." Low "dogs," on the other hand, have very flexible belief systems and are more easily influenced by new information or opinions.

Often it is difficult to communicate with students who are highly dogmatic. As far as they are concerned, they know the truth, and nothing the teacher says can alter that "truth" for them. Although students with this type of personality can be major problems in school, it should be recognized that parents and churches often go to great lengths to produce such closed-minded orientations. Virtually all religions are dogmatic; that is where the term *dogma* comes from. Dogma defines what is right and wrong, and children are taught to accept it on the basis of belief, not on the basis of demonstrable facts. Unfortunately, the beliefs of various groups are radically different from one another and are brought into the schools through the children of those groups. This can lead to hostile confrontations between students as well as between students and teachers. Although such problems cannot be completely avoided at all times, teachers are well served by the admonition to avoid striking one's head against a brick wall! Almost all groups seem to want "values education" in school, but they only want their own values included.

8 *Tolerance for Disagreement*   *SF*

As we have noted, people do not all think alike. Thus, there will be disagreements in school when students communicate with other students, teachers with other teachers, or teachers with students. Such disagreements cannot be avoided, nor should they be. *It is through disagreements and communication about such disagreements that new ideas are generated and better ways of doing things are learned.* A world without disagreement is a stagnant world.

Some people are able to deal with disagreement better than others. This ability involves an individual's level of "tolerance for disagreement"—*the degree to which we can deal with disagreement from another person before we take it personally.* Each person has a general level of tolerance, which is a traitlike personality variable. Beyond this, the situational consideration of who is being disagreeable comes into play. In general, we are more tolerant of disagreement from people we like than from people we dislike. However, people with a high personality-based tolerance for disagreement can handle disagreement even from people they do not like. By contrast, people with a low personality-based tolerance for disagreement cannot handle disagreement even from close friends.

When disagreement is taken personally, conflict is created. People with a high tolerance for disagreement, therefore, are relatively conflict resistant, while those with a low tolerance for disagreement are highly conflict prone. Teachers are well advised to work to increase their own tolerance for disagreement. Students will disagree, some almost constantly—particularly the kind of students we will talk about in the next section. The only way a teacher can avoid conflict with such students, therefore, is to modify her or his own behaviors.

Argumentativeness

Some people not only can tolerate disagreement, they thrive on it. They thoroughly enjoy arguing issues, even if it is just for the fun of it. They like to explore an issue until they are certain how they feel, even switching sides in the argument on occasion. Sometimes their method of attempting to influence others is to engage them in argument to get them to consider the new view. These people are considered high on the trait of argumentativeness.

Other people do not like arguing. If they have a low tolerance for disagreement, argumentativeness may make them feel personally attacked. They may resent the person who pushes them to argue more and may consider such a person abusive. They may see no value to argument at all. They are low on the trait of argumentativeness.

Argument does have value—probably less than high argumentatives believe, but more than thought by low argumentatives. It is valuable for students to explore different ways of looking at things, to take positions and attempt to defend them. Teachers need to take care, however, that such a valuable learning experience not be taken to extremes. Similarly, teachers need to be willing to defend the ideas they present in class, when these views are questioned by students, without taking such questioning personally and becoming defensive. Defensive reactions lead students to question the teacher's competence and the validity of what they are being taught.

We will not describe the many other personality variables that are believed to be associated with communication in the classroom. By looking at the limited number we have discussed, you can probably see that many aspects of personality come together to influence the communication behaviors of both teachers and students. In the remainder of this chapter, we will direct our attention to the personality orientation thought to have the most potent impact on communication behavior: communication apprehension. This is the most heavily researched personality variable in the communication field. Much of the research has been directed specifically toward the impact of communication apprehension in the classroom at all levels, from kindergarten through college.

The Nature of Communication Apprehension

Communication apprehension (CA) refers to an individual's level of fear or anxiety associated with either real or anticipated communication with another person or persons (McCroskey, 1977, 1984). People who are high in CA tend to get upset when forced to communicate and, as a result, try to avoid communication as much as possible. By contrast, people who are low in CA often enjoy communicating and commonly seek opportunities to communicate with others. Research indicates that this personality orientation is so strong for people at the high and low ends of the

CA continuum that it affects a large proportion of the important decisions these people must make in their lives, from what occupation to enter, to where to live, to whom to marry and when to do so.

Between 15 and 20 percent of the population—approximately one person in five—have been found to experience a dysfunctionally high level of CA. These people are not just bothered by some kinds of communication, they tend to be bothered to a significant extent by most kinds of communication. They experience fear and anxiety for which there is no rational explanation, and their apprehension gets in the way of their normal functioning in school, in the work environment, and socially.

Approximately the same proportion of the population are exceptionally low in CA. That is, these people are generally not bothered by any kind of communication. They do not experience fear or anxiety even when there is good reason for concern that communicating may not be in the person's best interest. Although such a lack of apprehension can be dangerous in some circumstances, communication is so highly valued and generally rewarded in U.S. society that these people are seldom at a disadvantage. It should be recognized that this may not be the case in some other cultures and societies. Thus, although our concern here is with people who are highly apprehensive, those who are not apprehensive may have serious problems in some other societies. As with all personality variables, there is no such thing as being on the "good end" of the CA continuum. What may be good in one culture may be dysfunctional in another.

Although one in five people experience the extremely apprehensive end of the CA continuum, many more experience CA in more restricted contexts. Almost everyone experiences communication apprehension to some degree under some circumstances—on a job interview, on a first date, while serving on a committee, when talking with one's boss, or while asking or answering a question in a class. Or CA may occur in the most common situation for experiencing it—public speaking. More than 70 percent of the U.S. population report experiencing communication apprehension, more commonly called stage fright, when giving a public speech. In fact, surveys have determined that giving a public speech is Americans' number-one fear! (Fear of death comes in third.) So if you hear people say they would rather die than give a public speech, they may be telling you the truth!

Clarifying Distinctions

To avoid confusion, it is useful to make several distinctions between CA as a trait-like personality orientation and other things that are similar or related. We will consider four of these here.

Trait versus Transitory CA

Trait CA is more than the common phenomenon of being fearful or anxious about a particular communication event. It is a personality orientation that affects the totality of the individual's world. Many of the important choices we have to make in life involve communication, or the potential for communication. Trait CA can influence any or all of those choices. The apprehension we experience about a particular communication event, on the other hand, is transitory. When the event passes, so do the feelings, unpleasant as they may be at the time. Although such an experience may lead us to avoid very similar situations in the future, it is very unlikely to have any wider implications for our life. By contrast, trait CA doesn't go away, nor do its effects on our life as a whole.

CA versus General Anxiety

General anxiety relates to a personality orientation (discussed earlier in this chapter) that leads people to be fearful or anxious about a wide variety of factors in their lives—taking chances, being evaluated, snakes, birds, earthquakes, weather, driving, leaving the house, and so on. CA relates only to communication. It is only communication or the prospect of communication that results in the fearful or anxious response. A person who is generally anxious is likely to experience anxiety in some communication situations as well. However, a person with high CA is no more likely to be fearful or anxious about things that do not involve communication than is anyone who does not have high CA. The key to remember is that CA relates only to communication; general anxiety relates to everything.

Trait versus Context-Based CA

Trait CA is related to virtually all communication in which a person might find her- or himself. Context-based CA is related to only one type of communication context, such as public speaking, talking in large meetings or classes, talking in small groups, talking in dyads, job interviews, asserting oneself, arguing with someone, and so on. The person with high trait CA is likely to be bothered in all, or nearly all, of these contexts. It is quite possible, however, for a person to be bothered by one, or only a few, types of context. A person can have severe stage fright about giving a speech but have no problem at all with talking in groups. Similarly, a person can be very shy and apprehensive about talking in dyads but not be bothered by public speaking. In fact, this is true of many professional communicators such as television and radio personalities, trial lawyers, ministers, actors and actresses, and even teachers. The fact that a person is apprehensive about one type of communication context does not mean he or she is a high CA.

Trait versus Receiver-Based CA

There are many different types of receivers. Trait CA involves communicating with all, or virtually all, types of receivers. Receiver-based CA involves communication with only one or a few general types of receivers, such as strangers, acquaintances, friends, supervisors, older people, young people, people from particular ethnic groups, and so on. It is common for a person to be very apprehensive about talking to strangers but not bothered at all by talking to friends.

The senior author had an experience several years ago that really brought home to him the importance of this distinction. He was serving as a member of the examination committee of a student who was completing her final oral exam for her master's degree. She was very obviously terrified, so much so that she had difficulty answering very simple questions—ones for which she obviously knew the answers, since she had already answered them on a written exam. Knowing that she taught third grade, he indicated that he noticed her present anxiety and asked her how she could tolerate teaching third graders all day, every day. She acknowledged her current fear and contrasted the situation with her normal teaching experience by noting that teaching third graders "isn't like talking to real people!"

Undoubtedly, her anxious state influenced her choice of words, but the choice really made the point. She was not a high trait CA; she was only bothered by some kinds of people, like her examining committee. Even after we informed her that she had passed, she still appeared to be a nervous wreck! Teachers should remember how they are seen by many students. Even though some students may talk up a storm on the playground or in the hallway, one should not be surprised to find them scared to death to talk in front of the teacher. To expect such a student to volunteer to talk in class is expecting far too much, and calling on that student is the communication equivalent of child abuse.

Causes of Trait Communication Apprehension

When research on CA was in its early years, scholars regularly dismissed any possibility that CA could be caused by a genetic factor. After the results of major studies involving the personalities of twins were published, however, it was no longer possible to discount the biological influence of genetics on temperament. It now seems clear that when babies are born, they differ from one another on certain temperament and personality tendencies. Although no one would claim that all personality is totally genetically determined, it is clear that babies are born with predispositions toward certain personality orientations.

We have used the terms *personality* and *temperament*. It is important that we clarify the distinction between them. Personality refers to specific trait predispositions toward behavior, such as Machiavellianism and dogmatism. Researchers have identified more than 2,000 such traits. To get a better understanding of this extremely large number of traits, psychologists have identified "super traits." Most of the individual personality traits are correlated with one or more of these super traits, which are also referred to as "temperaments."

Different researchers have proposed the existence of between 3 and 16 temperament variables. Most of the work in this area has focused on two temperament classifications, commonly known as the "big 3" and the "big 5." The big 3 are extraversion, neuroticism, and psychoticism (Eysenck, 1990). The big 5 are extraversion, neuroticism, agreeableness, openness to experience, and conscientiousness (Costa & McCrae, 1992). It is generally accepted that these temperament variables—like most, if not all, personality traits—are a function of genetically produced systems in the brain. Research in communication has found these temperament variables to be highly correlated with communication traits, such as CA and willingness to communicate. Psychobiologists indicate that the primary manifestations of temperaments are communication behaviors. Hence, it is believed that communication traits are caused by the same brain systems that produce temperament.

The implications of this research are very important to our understanding of such communication traits as CA. Because these traits have a strong genetic base, it is very difficult, if not impossible, to change them. Several learning-based methods of reducing CA have been developed. Although they have been found to be of some help, particularly for people who have very high CA, the observed positive effects have been quite small.

Effects of Communication Apprehension

There are four distinct, though not unrelated, effects that can be produced by high CA: internal discomfort, communication avoidance, communication withdrawal, and overcommunication. Each of these effects can be observed in most classrooms, although few students manifest all four.

Internal Discomfort

The only effect of CA that is universal across both individuals and types of CA is an internally experienced feeling of discomfort. High physiological arousal is common in many communication situations. People who are low in CA interpret this arousal as excitement. These people channel their excitement into the act of communicating and regularly report it to be helpful to them. By contrast, people with high CA interpret this arousal as fear. This perception tends to increase the arousal even more, and this fear–arousal–fear cycle sometimes escalates to the point where the person is terrified.

The cognitive response to real or anticipated communication, then, can range from mild concern to abject terror, with a variety of physiological changes being produced as well. Blood pressure may increase, heart rate may go up, more perspiration may occur, the hands may tremble, the voice may quake, the mouth may go dry. In extreme cases, fainting may occur.

Excessive arousal, then, can have a very debilitating impact on a communicator, just as it can on an athlete. Although an athlete must be aroused to a certain level to perform well, excessive activation may cause poor performance. Excessive arousal may cause athletes to do such things as jump offside in football, shoot a basketball too hard or soft (getting an "air ball"), have a false start in track or swimming, miss the target completely in shooting sports, or throw a gutter ball in bowling. Both athletes and public speakers have been known to regurgitate just before they perform or, worse, while they are performing. More commonly, communicators forget what they want to talk about, their hands shake so much that they cannot read their notes, and their mouths go so dry they can barely speak. Students who know or believe they are going to have to communicate have great difficulty learning new information in class. They concentrate so much on trying to figure out how to cope with the communication demands that they may learn little of what the teacher is trying to teach.

Such experiences, though unpleasant, are usually not terminal. In some cases, however, people have actually had heart attacks and died while giving a public speech. Such an extreme reaction is uncommon but not unheard of. More commonly, particularly in the classroom context, students who are bothered by communication find ways to get themselves out of having to communicate. They simply do not experience the extreme internal discomfort because it is so aversive it forces them to choose between the options of "fight or flight." Overwhelmingly, their choice is to flee through one of the next two possible effects of CA—avoidance or withdrawal. If these avenues are cut off by a well-meaning but ignorant teacher, the extreme reactions we've noted are likely to occur. And, of course, if the reactions are severe enough and a student is injured in any way, this opens the teacher to possible legal consequences.

Communication Avoidance   SF

Most people who have high CA, either trait, context-based, or receiver-based, have the extreme type of experience described here no more than once, if at all. The experience is so traumatic, or they foresee it as being so traumatic, that they take the steps necessary to be sure it does not happen again. They avoid situations where the feared communication might be required. Often without even being fully conscious that they are doing so, people with high CA arrange their lives in such a way that the chance of being forced into the feared communication is reduced to a very minimal level.

Research in this area has uncovered many such avoidance methods. For example, it has been found that people with high CA choose housing that is in more remote areas, even in such areas as dormitories and apartment buildings. They go into occupations that they believe have low communication demands. They refuse (typical of females) or do not ask for (typical of males) dates. They do not show up for job interviews.

In school, the people with high CA do not sign up for classes known to require communication, unless the course itself is required. They drop classes when they learn part of the grade is on "class participation." They simply stay home sick on days when they are expected to perform for show and tell, current events, book reports, science projects, or other public speaking activities. They choose majors that do not have classes that require such communication performances. They prefer large lecture classes over small, interactive classes, and enroll in those larger classes when possible.

Communication Withdrawal

Sometimes it is not possible for a person to avoid communication altogether. Communication demands sometimes arise unexpectedly. People with high CA are then forced to resort to the other "flight" response—to withdraw as quickly and fully as possible. Sometimes this can be done physically, by actual physical departure. In other cases it is accomplished psychologically, by tuning out to what is going on or by minimizing one's participation.

Research has indicated that a variety of options are employed to accomplish withdrawal. Students may choose seats at the sides or in the back of the room, where they are least likely to be called upon. In small groups, they try to sit in an inconspicuous place where attention is less likely to be directed toward them. Some will simply say, "I don't know," when asked a question—even if they do know. Another effective dodge is to respond with irrelevant comments when called upon. After a few of these responses, virtually no one will bother the student again! Of course, these students do not raise their hands to participate even when they do know the answer.

Overcommunication

A small minority of students with high CA choose the final option. They decide to fight rather than flee. These people go out of their way to place themselves in communication situations in the hope that, with enough practice, they can beat the CA problem. Often, the behaviors these people engage in are so inappropriate for a person who is afraid of communication that others may think they are actually low in CA.

Students who choose this "fight" option may voluntarily register for a public speaking course or even join the debating team or drama club. They may run for a student office. They may volunteer to serve as chair of a committee. They may raise their hand to answer a question in class, even if they have no idea of the answer. They tend to force themselves into the conversations of others. Not surprisingly, these are the very people who are sometimes thought to "talk too much." As we have noted, it is not the quantity of their talk that is problematic, but its negative quality.

Although it is rare that a person can take on CA and come out the victor, some people claim they have been victorious in such battles. In most instances, however, these people were never really high in the CA trait. Rather, they were moderate in terms of the CA trait but were bothered by one or more context-based or receiver-based concerns. Through practice and/or study, they became better in their problem area(s) and simply overestimate the amount they have changed.

Changing traits of any kind is difficult and normally requires the assistance of a trained professional. It is possible, however, for teachers to help students who are high in CA. They may not be able help students reduce their levels of trait CA, but they can become part of the solution instead of part of the problem. That is, they can do things in their classrooms so that highly apprehensive students will have an easier time coping with their CA while maximizing their opportunity to learn. To conclude this chapter, we will consider five of these ways that teachers can help.

Preventing and Reducing CA Problems in the Classroom

It is quite possible for a teacher to make a classroom more comfortable for the 1 student in 5 who is high in CA. Since that is equivalent to 5 students even in a relatively small class of 25, it is well worth the teacher's time and effort. There are five general methods for helping these students that are quite simple to implement. Let us consider each.

Reduce Oral Communication Demands   *DW*

With the exception of classes on public speaking and oral foreign language, talk need not be a focal activity in the classroom for all students. Communication demands can be reduced without sacrificing learning by doing the following:

1. *Avoid testing through talk.* There are many ways for students to demonstrate that they have learned material (taking written tests, drawing pictures, performing given tasks, and so on). Even oral reading is not necessary to determine whether a student can read. All it tests is oral performance ability. Be certain that what you are testing is what is learned, not how little can be remembered by a high CA forced to talk.

2. *Avoid grading based on participation.* In spite of what teachers continue to say (and probably believe), research indicates that what is graded in most cases is quantity of participation, not quality. Grading based on talking directly handicaps one student in five. Not only will those students be unlikely to talk anyway, unless forced to do so, they will be so worried about communication that their concern will interfere with their learning. If participation is required because it is assumed to enhance learning, that is a false assumption for many students.

3. *Avoid alphabetical seating.* This type of seating offers little advantage, other than a minor convenience for taking roll. It has the high potential for placing a high-CA student right in the areas with the highest communication demands. Research indicates that this approach will not increase their communication, but it will reduce their learning. To the extent you can given the level of instruction you are dealing with, let students select their own seats so that they do not end up in high-interaction areas if they do not want to. You can always have the students put their names on the seating chart so you can take roll, even if it is not alphabetical.

4. *Avoid randomly calling on students to respond.* This procedure drives students who are afraid to communicate up the wall and, more important, reduces their learning by causing them to worry about being forced to communicate rather than pay attention to the lesson.

None of these suggestions requires any major change in the instructional system, yet they all can contribute to making the classroom a more comfortable place for learning by reducing oral communication demands. It must be stressed here that it is the demands for oral communication that are being reduced, not the oral communication. None of these suggestions in any way interfere with students who want to communicate.

Make Communication a Rewarding Experience

Although you are not likely to change a student's trait CA level by doing so, you can help the student see your classroom as a context in which he or she may feel comfortable communicating. This can be done, and has been, by many teachers who have made the effort to do so. Here are some suggestions.

1. *Praise students when they participate, particularly the quiet ones.* It seems so obvious that if we want students to communicate we should praise communication. But observation indicates that many teachers really do not do this. Even if the student with high CA says nothing for weeks, simply observing that others are praised when they talk increases the likelihood that the high-CA student will eventually do so, too.

2. *Try to avoid indicating that any answer is completely "wrong" when given in class.* This is sometimes difficult, but it is worth trying to accomplish. Find something positive about the answer, even if it is something like: "That answer is not completely correct, but it is one of the answers most commonly given. Let's look at how we can improve on it." This approach reduces the risk factor for being wrong.

3. *Try not to punish any student for talking.* If students are disruptive, make it very clear to everyone that it is the disruption that is being punished. Continue to encourage the student who was punished to participate. This will help make it clear that communication is valued in your classroom.

4. *Never enforce quietness as a punishment.* That's right—never. There are plenty of other things that can be used for punishment. Instead, take a positive stance by using communication itself as a reward. When students have been good or have done something well, allow them to talk to each other for a few minutes as a reward.

These methods will lead students with high CA to perceive communication in a more positive light, and communicating in your classroom as less threatening. Even though they may continue to avoid communication in other classrooms, you may convince them that it is OK to talk in your class, even if only occasionally. After all, a little communication is better than none.

Be Consistent about Communication

Remember, stress is generated by inconsistent rewards, by the absence of rewards, and by punishments. Here are some ways to reduce the potential for stress:

1. *Try to be consistent in how you handle student talk.* Try to make sure that students can be certain of your response before they speak, so that they do not get unexpected responses, particularly negative ones, to their talk.

2. *Be very clear about any rules you must have regarding talking.* Don't use your judgment; check with the students for their perceptions. It is those perceptions that count! Give everyone at least one chance to break a talk rule before being punished, and give the quiet ones even more chances. They don't need to be conditioned even more to believe that talk and punishment go together.

Reduce Ambiguity, Novelty, and Evaluation

Uncertainty makes people uncomfortable, and that discomfort is even worse for students who are high in CA, because those students do not have the luxury of asking questions to clear things up. Thus, you should do the following:

1. *Make all assignments as clear and unambiguous as you can.* Give all students the opportunity to ask questions about assignments. Although the student with high CA is not likely to ask these questions, others may do so, allowing the apprehensive student to get the answer without having to ask the question.

2. *Make certain all students understand how they will be evaluated.* Do not place too much emphasis on the evaluation of any type of talk.

3. *Avoid surprises.* It is fine to change the way you do things, but do not put the student on the spot for not understanding the new system. Remember, the student with high CA will usually accept failure rather than communicate in order to succeed.

Increase Student Control over Success

Students who feel that they are in control of how well they will do in a class have confidence. Confident students are more likely to communicate than those who lack confidence. To help give students confidence, you may be able to do the following:

1. *Give students options.* The more options students have, the more they can select options that fit their own style of learning. Students with high CA can avoid those options that require a lot of communication.

2. *Be certain that a student can avoid communication and still do well in the course.* If the term project in the course requires an oral presentation and counts for one-third of the final grade, students with high CA will feel helpless. If possible, then, allow students to present that project in writing, or to do some other type of project altogether.

Although each of the suggestions in the five areas described here may require you to do some things a little differently than you have in the past, none represent such a dramatic change that you should have major difficulty following them. More complex suggestions for helping apprehensive students are readily available should you wish to learn about them (McCroskey & Richmond, 1991; this book may be accessed at no cost at www.jamescmccroskey.com/publications/booksg/booksg21.pdf).

The term *sensitivity* has probably been overused in recent years, but it is appropriate here. If you are sensitive to how your teaching behaviors might be perceived by your apprehensive students, you will probably have little trouble becoming part of the solution. If you are insensitive to how those students perceive your behaviors, you will continue to be part of the problem.

References

Costa, P. T., & McCrae, R. R. (1992). *NEO-PI-R: Revised personality inventory.* Odessa, FL: Psychological Assessment Resources.

Eysenck, H. J. (1990). Biological dimensions of personality. In L. A. Pervin (Ed.), *Handbook of personality: Theory and research* (pp. 244–276). New York: Guilford.

McCroskey, J. C. (1977). Oral communication apprehension: A summary of recent theory and research. *Human Communication Research, 4,* 78–96.

McCroskey, J. C. (1984). The communication apprehension perspective. In J. A. Daly & J. C. McCroskey (Eds.), *Avoiding communication: Shyness, reticence, and communication apprehension* (pp. 13–38). Beverly Hills, CA: Sage.

McCroskey, J. C., & Daly, J. A. (Eds.). (1987). *Personality and interpersonal communication.* Newbury Park, CA: Sage.

McCroskey, J. C., & Richmond, V. P. (1991). *Quiet children and the classroom teacher,* 2nd ed. Bloomington, IN: ERIC Clearinghouse on Reading and Communication Skills, and Annandale, VA: Speech Communication Association.

Glossary

argumentativeness   The degree to which an individual enjoys arguing about ideas with others and being good at presenting and defending her or his own ideas as well as disputing the ideas of others.

basic attribution error   The tendency for individuals to attribute their own good behavior to their personality and their own bad behavior to situations, while tending to attribute others' good behavior to situations and others' bad behavior to their personalities.

big 3   The dimensions of temperament according to Eysenck (1990): extraversion, neuroticism, and psychoticism.

big 5   The dimensions of temperament according to Costa and McCrae (1992): extraversion, neuroticism, agreeableness, openness to experience, and conscientiousness.

communication apprehension   An individual's level of fear or anxiety associated with either real or anticipated communication with another person or persons.

dogmatism   The degree of rigidity of a person's belief system.

general anxiety   Also known as "neuroticism." The tendency to be fearful of many things in one's environment, including things that there is no rational reason to fear.

internal discomfort   The only universal effect of communication apprehension. It may be manifested by such factors as elevated blood pressure, increased heart rate, trembling hands, increased perspiration, quaking voice, and/or dry mouth.

locus of control   Attribution of the cause of what influences a person's successes and/or failures. Those with an external locus of control believe that chance, luck, or God determines the outcomes in their lives. Those with an internal locus of control believe that their own behaviors determine the outcomes in their lives.

Machiavellian   Personality characteristic of an individual who enjoys manipulating other people and typically is skilled at doing so.

personality   The sum total of an individual's characteristics that make her or him unique.

public-speaking anxiety   Fear or anxiety associated with either real or anticipated presentation of a public speech; the number-one fear of adults in the United States.

self-concept   The way a person sees her- or himself.

self-esteem   The way a person evaluates her- or himself.

"talks too much"   A quantitative description of a wide variety of qualitative problems observed in another person's communication behavior.

tolerance for disagreement   The degree to which an individual can deal with disagreement from another person before taking it personally.

12

Teacher Communication Traits and Student Perceptions

In Chapters 10 and 11, we examined several communication traits of students that can have a bearing on how well they are likely to do in the classroom. Equally important are the traits that teachers and trainers bring into the classroom. In fact, these communication traits may have an even greater impact on student learning than do the traits of the students.

Teacher Communication Traits

Like students and all other adults, teachers vary greatly in their communication trait orientations. They also differ in terms of their temperament traits and their personality traits. It is often argued that some people are born to be great teachers. Although this is not a universal truth, it certainly is true that some people's temperament and personality traits make it more likely that they will become great teachers. We will examine here some of the communication-related traits that seem to be most closely associated with effective or ineffective teaching. These include the temperament traits of extraversion and neuroticism and the communication-related traits of willingness to communicate, communication apprehension, self-perceived communication competence, compulsive communication, tolerance for disagreement, argumentativeness, and verbal aggressiveness.

Extraversion

Teachers who are high on extraversion are more outgoing and willing to communicate with their students than teachers who are more introverted. Extraverted teachers enjoy communicating with their students. Introverted teachers, on the other hand, prefer to be away from their students. They do not enjoy talking with them and hence have fewer interactions with students than more extraverted teachers do. Extraverted teachers are seen as "student friendly"; introverted teachers are not.

Neuroticism

Neuroticism is associated with emotional control and anxiety. Neurotic teachers may be unsure of their capacity to communicate effectively with their students. Hence, they are less likely to initiate communication with students. They also may discourage communication, both in the classroom and outside of class. Nonneurotic teachers have more control over their emotions and, as a result, are more comfortable communicating with their students and less likely to get into conflicts with them. Many of the communication-related traits that are associated with teacher effectiveness are related to both extraversion and neuroticism.

Willingness to Communicate

As we have noted previously, willingness to communicate manifests itself primarily in one's willingness to initiate communication with others. It is positively associated with extraversion and negatively associated with neuroticism. Teachers who are highly willing to communicate are likely to encourage communication with their students, both in class and outside of class. Because people must communicate to develop positive relationships, these teachers are more likely to develop good relationships with their students. By contrast, those who are not willing to communicate will typically have more distant relationships with their students and will seldom communicate with them outside of the classroom environment.

Communication Apprehension

One in five teachers are highly apprehensive about communication. They are introverted neurotics. These teachers usually will try to develop a classroom environment in which they will have little interaction with their students. This is less true for teachers at the lower grade levels, but more likely to be true in high school, college, and adult learner contexts. Communication apprehension reduces the probability of developing good communication relationships with students at any level.

Self-Perceived Communication Competence

Teachers who see themselves as more competent communicators are extraverted nonneurotics. They are confident about their own communication and are open to and comfortable with communication with students. They are likely to have higher self-esteem and are unlikely to be intimidated by their students. Teachers who have low levels of self-perceived communication competence typically have lower self-esteem. All of this combines to make them less willing to get involved in communication with their students. As a result, their students may see them as less friendly and may become less willing to interact with these teachers.

Compulsive Communication

Compulsive communicators are driven to communicate. They are often referred to as "talkaholics." Teachers who are compulsive communicators will engage in a lot of communication with their students, both within and outside the classroom. Because of their high affinity for communication, they may tend to dominate the interaction in the classroom and may sometimes get carried away with classroom discussions. These teachers are very high on extraversion but are neither high nor low on neuroticism.

Tolerance for Disagreement

Disagreement is very common in many classroom environments, particularly those above the elementary school level. In many classrooms, such disagreements form the foundation of much of the classroom communication. Being tolerant of students who disagree with her or his opinions is a very positive characteristic in a teacher. Tolerant teachers not only encourage disagreement on the part of students but also manage not to be hypercritical of those who disagree with them. Teachers with low tolerance for disagreement often stifle differences of opinion in their classes and sometimes react very negatively when their own opinions are not shared by the students. Teachers who have high tolerance for disagreement are more extraverted and somewhat higher on psychoticism (that is, they are not committed to traditional norms) than others.

Argumentativeness

Teachers who are highly argumentative are very much like teachers with high tolerance for disagreement. They are more extraverted and somewhat higher on psychoticism. They tend to enjoy arguing with others, even "just for the fun of it." They are likely to state a disagreement with someone else even if they actually agree with what the other person says. They enjoy a clash of ideas. Although this characteristic is for the most part a positive one for a teacher, because it tends to initiate lively classroom discussions and debates, it can also be negative. Teachers must be careful not to challenge too strongly the views of students who are low argumentatives and who, therefore, often react with verbal aggression when their ideas are challenged. Teachers who are low in argumentativeness also need to be careful how they respond to students who disagree with what they say, since their normal tendency is to verbally attack people who disagree with them.

Verbal Aggressiveness

Teachers who are verbally aggressive are neither high nor low on either extraversion or neuroticism. However, they are higher than most on psychoticism. In part, psychoticism involves being less concerned about the feelings of others. Hence, verbal aggressiveness can be a serious problem for teachers. Verbal aggression substitutes attacks on other people's character for attacks on their ideas. Although in some communication contexts, verbal aggression may have some positive characteristics, the classroom is not such a context. When teachers are verbally aggressive with students, it is common that the teacher–student relationship becomes very negative. Hence, verbally aggressive teachers need to control such communication behavior in the classroom very carefully.

In Appendix A of this book, several measures are provided that you can use as self-diagnoses of the communication traits you have. You may find it helpful to complete and score these measures to see if any of your communication traits may cause you trouble as a classroom teacher or trainer.

Student Perceptions and Student Realities

We have all been taught in some part of our educational experience that perception is not reality. In other words, the way we see the world may not be what the world really is. From a communication vantage point, we have to qualify this general position. The perceptions students have of their teachers *are* the students' realities. That is, what you as a teacher really are and do is not necessarily what your students see you as being or see you as doing. Students react to teachers on the basis of what they see the teacher as being and doing, and also on the basis of all of their own prejudices, biases, and previous experiences. Although we might wish that their perceptions would be based purely on what we really are and do, that is not necessarily what happens. Students' perceptions are their realities.

Research in the field of instructional communication has identified four student perceptions of teachers that are substantially associated with their affect toward both the teacher and the content taught, as well as the students' motivation to learn the content from the teacher and the degree to which students perceive they have learned the content. All four perceptions are communication based. These perceptions are (1) whether the teacher is clear, (2) whether the teacher is immediate, (3) whether the teacher is assertive, and (4) whether the teacher is responsive. We will consider each of these.

1. *Clarity.* Clarity has to do with whether the teacher communicates the material in a way that makes it understandable (as opposed to confusing). Clarity is a critical factor in students' perceptions of the quality of instruction to which they are exposed. It involves numerous teacher communication behaviors, such as the use of voice, rate of speaking, whether the teacher's accent can be understood, the number and quality of examples the teacher provides, and so on.

2. *Immediacy.* Immediacy has to do with students' perceptions of their psychological closeness to the teacher. This phenomenon is produced predominantly by nonverbal communication behaviors (discussed in detail in Chapter 14). Students prefer teachers who are immediate with their students.

3. *Assertiveness.* Assertive teachers have control of their classroom without being authoritarian or abusive toward their students. They are seen as leading the class and "being on top of things." This should not be confused with aggressiveness. Assertive teachers insist on commanding the respect and control normally expected in the learning environment. Aggressive teachers go well beyond the norm in terms of their demands on students and are often seen as abusive. Assertive teachers are viewed as being independent, forceful, dominant, and willing to take a stand.

4. *Responsiveness.* Responsiveness has to do with paying attention to student needs and, when necessary, adapting to those needs. Being a good listener is an important part of being seen by students as responsive. Responsive teachers are perceived as helpful, sincere, friendly, and compassionate.

Teachers' communication behaviors, both verbal and nonverbal, influence these student perceptions—and ultimately the students' quality of learning. In Appendix B of this book, measures of each of these perceptions are provided. You are free to copy these measures and have your students complete them in your class. They can help you spot potential problems in the perceptions that your students may have of you as a teacher so that you can try to improve those perceptions.

Glossary

assertiveness   The ability to stand up for oneself and not let others take advantage of oneself, without taking advantage of others.

clarity   Communicating in such a way that material is immediately understandable to students.

compulsive communicators   Individuals who are driven to communicate, also known as "talkaholics."

immediacy   The perception students have of their teacher's physical or psychological closeness to them.

responsiveness   The ability to be sensitive to the needs, feelings, and communication of others and to be a good listener.

talkaholics   See "compulsive communicators."

verbal aggressiveness   The tendency of some individuals, when engaged in disagreement or argument with others, to personally attack (verbally) the other person rather than focus on the issue under discussion.

13

Teacher Behaviors

What Students Like and Dislike

Upon receiving an unsatisfactory teaching review, a lecturer in the junior author's department asked for clarification as to why the committee gave this rating. Unfortunately, this department emphasizes the course evaluations provided by the students each semester—especially the question that focuses on the overall effectiveness of the teacher. The lecturer believed that her evaluations must be actually very high in comparison with those of others teaching similar courses in the department (the averages are compared across all courses taught during a term). She expressed surprise when it was explained to her that several professors in the department received perfect, or nearly perfect, scores on this item. It was hard for her to understand and accept that her assumption that her ratings were among the highest was not accurate.

Since the lecturer knew that the junior author's ratings did rank among the highest in the department, she asked, "So, what is it that you do that makes your students evaluate you so highly?" A preferred question might have been, "What is it that you do to enhance student learning?" An even better question for her to ask would have been, "What *don't* you do in the classroom?" That is actually the question that was answered. It was explained to her why certain behaviors are not advantageous for achieving student learning outcomes and high effectiveness ratings.

Up to this point in the book, we have not examined less-than-desirable teacher behaviors as determined by the students. This chapter focuses solely on teacher behavior in the classroom from the vantage point of student expectations and perceptions of the appropriateness and desirability of those behaviors. Of primary importance is the impact that teacher misbehavior has on learning outcomes. We will begin by examining a stream of research that identifies specific teacher misbehaviors. We will then direct our attention to student perceptions in the intercultural classroom context (classrooms in which teachers are perceived to be culturally dissimilar to their students).

Teacher Misbehaviors

We all are aware that sometimes students will misbehave in the classroom, even at the college level. Sometimes these students are aware that their behavior is inappropriate, and sometimes they simply have not learned the norms for that particular classroom environment. Other factors are also influential in why students may misbehave in the classroom. Among those reasons are low motivation to learn, laziness, poor socioeconomic background, difficulties at home, and so on. These misbehaviors can be detrimental to learning.

Teachers are the same as students in many respects. Some teachers are trained to teach, while unfortunately other teachers have no formal training and are sent into a pack of wolves to fend for themselves. However, some of those teachers, both trained and untrained, may understand *how* they are supposed to behave in the classroom but still enact behaviors that are not only inappropriate from an administrative or learning perspective, but also perceived to be undesirable from the student's perspective. For some of the same reasons that students misbehave, teachers misbehave. But recent research suggests that there are some other, less obvious reasons why teachers may misbehave in the classroom.

Kearney, Plax, and Allen (2002) contend that teachers misbehave because they are too self-focused, worrying excessively about whether they will come across as credible, competent, and intelligent. Other teachers simply feel justified in misbehaving as a function of their position. It is important to note that, regardless of the reason for teacher misbehavior, the effect is harmful to students.

Reasons Why Teachers Misbehave

As we have suggested, sometimes teachers know they are misbehaving, but sometimes they have no idea that their behavior is perceived as misbehavior. New teachers may desire a list of "what not to do in the classroom." But such a list is useful only if the teacher understands *why* the behaviors are bad. This situation is similar to that of travelers sojourning in a foreign country. They may have found a list of "dos and don'ts" for behaving—for example, to bow rather than to shake hands upon meeting a person in Japan. The depth of the bow indicates the other person's status, among its many other relational meanings. To bow in this context is appropriate, but the nuances of the bow must also be understood if the bow is to be performed correctly. In the classroom, a teacher may know that it is important to deliver an organized lecture but may not understand that lack of certain immediate behaviors while giving the lecture can lead to perceptions of incompetence, uncaring feelings toward the students, reduced cognitive learning, and so on. It is therefore important to identify some common teacher misbehaviors and then to explain their implications for the classroom.

Kearney et al. (2002) content-analyzed college students' descriptions of specific instances in which a teacher said or did something to irritate, demotivate, or distract them during a course. They coded the descriptions into 28 different categories and grouped each into three dimensions of teacher-misbehavior profiles. The most commonly cited types of misbehavior were sarcasm or put-downs, early dismissal, straying from the subject, unfair testing, and boring lectures. A few others were confusing/unclear lectures, unresponsiveness to students' questions, having a foreign or regional accent, and imposing unreasonable and arbitrary rules. Underlying these misbehaviors were three teacher profiles: incompetent, offensive, and indolent. The authors describe the profiles in the following ways (p. 129).

1. *Incompetent.* Incompetent teachers engage in a cluster of misbehaviors that indicate to students that the teacher doesn't care about either the course or the student. These teachers don't bother to learn their students' names, make their tests too difficult, and are unable or unwilling to help their students succeed. Above all, incompetent teachers are simply bad lecturers: They either bore or confuse their students; some overload them with too much information; and still others mispronounce words or engage in accented speech that the students cannot understand.

2. *Offensive.* Offensive teachers are mean, cruel, and/or ugly in their behavior. They humiliate students, play favorites, intimidate, and are generally condescending, rude, and self-centered. Offensive teachers can be sarcastic, verbally abusive, arbitrary, and unreasonable.

3. *Indolent.* Finally, indolent teachers are reminiscent of the absent-minded professor. They sometimes fail to show up for class, or they may arrive late; they forget test dates, neglect to grade homework, constantly readjust assignments, and/or underwhelm students by making their classes and tests too easy.

Obviously, no teacher enacts all of the misbehaviors in these profiles. You can take an inventory of some of the misbehaviors of which you are guilty. You might try to justify reasons for your misbehaviors by using an external locus of control or by attributing the behavior to the situation. You might wonder if there is ever a situation in which misbehaving can be positive. Here is an example of teacher misbehavior, but it is not suggested that teachers emulate this exercise.

An Example of a Teacher Misbehaving

This teacher purposefully misbehaves in the classroom for one standard lecture in order to arouse student anxiety in the classroom and to introduce the communication apprehension (CA) construct. It is noted frequently during the beginning of each term, and also on the syllabus, that students will never be forced to get up in front of the class alone to make an impromptu presentation. Around midterm, the students are asked to prepare an introduction to a formal seminar topic that they have been researching. They have roughly four minutes to prepare (they need only to present an attention-getter, a statement of relevancy, a credibility statement, or a preview of points). As time is counted down in 30-second intervals, the teacher does not smile, does not establish eye contact, and is vocally nonimmediate. Essentially, the teacher is being mean!

The students see the sharp contrast with normal behavior, all the while internalizing stress and manifesting nervous behaviors. Two students are called on and, one by one, offer reasons that they should not be the first to present (e.g., they volunteered, they are female or male, or some other very arbitrary excuse). When the third student is called to the podium, the three students are asked if they were present during the first week of class. Then they are asked to recall what had been announced regarding impromptu speaking in the class. If they don't recall, someone else in the class invariably speaks out: "That we will never have to do them!" At this point, the students are asked why they are standing up front when, in fact, no one will be forced to give an introduction. And then they are told that the lecture topic for the day is anxiety!

The collective sigh of relief seemingly could trigger a car alarm in the parking lot. After the students have relaxed from all this, the reasons for the teacher misbehaviors that they have just experienced are explained. Although the students frequently indicate that they were very upset during the experience, they typically also indicate that the whole thing is behind them now and that they are just happy that they don't have to get up to speak!

Such violations of student expectations for teacher behavior can be disastrous, particularly when the teacher is not even aware that he or she is misbehaving. Most teachers, at one time or another, will misbehave in some fashion. The key is to recognize what teacher behaviors are seen as misbehaviors, try to avoid those behaviors to the extent possible, and learn how to deal with those problems when they arise. We will provide a list of suggestions for dealing with misbehaviors at the end of this chapter.

Relationships of Misbehaviors with Perceived Immediacy, Caring, and Student Anxiety

As alluded to previously, teachers sometimes send unintentionally negative messages. Under normal circumstances, most teachers do not purposefully misbehave. However, Thweatt and McCroskey (1996) examined nonimmediate teacher behaviors and discovered that students perceived these nonimmediate behaviors to be misbehaviors. Nonimmediacy cues have been viewed as nothing more than the opposite of immediacy cues. Immediacy cues serve to reduce perceived distance between people. They either truly reduce physical distance, or they reduce the psychological distance. Immediate behaviors include such things as smiling, making eye contact, moving within the classroom, touching, and many other elements of nonverbal communication.

Immediacy has been the focus of a considerable amount of research in which it was found that immediacy has positive impacts in the classroom. For example, students have been shown to have more positive affect for teachers high in immediacy, which leads to increased affective learning (Richmond, McCroskey,

Plax, & Kearney, 1986). Dolin (1995) suggested that nonimmediate communication behaviors clearly interfere with student learning and thus may be perceived as misbehaviors. Thweatt and McCroskey (1996) found that otherwise nonmisbehaving teachers who were nonimmediate were perceived as misbehaving. They concluded: "Teachers who, either by choice or ignorance, fail to engage in immediate behaviors are misbehaving, at least in the eyes of their students. This may explain why students perceive the nonimmediate teacher, who functions in an otherwise efficient manner, less positively than the immediate teacher who may not even be efficient in accomplishing his/her duties" (p. 204). In their studies, students evaluated the nonimmediate teacher as engaging in a high level of misbehavior, even if that teacher was credited with otherwise only appropriate behavior.

The implications of this work are very salient for teachers. Simply doing one's job correctly is not enough. Teachers must make students comfortable about approaching them and must assure students that they—the teachers—are comfortable with approaching students. Creating a feeling of immediacy ensures that the teacher who may be forced to engage in what students perceive to be inappropriate behaviors on occasion will not lose the positive affect of the students.

Immediacy is related to perceived caring. Perceived caring has a positive relationship with student learning and teacher evaluation. As discussed in Chapter 7, the source credibility dimension of "goodwill" is important to student learning. Perceived caring is closely associated with goodwill. Further, three factors are believed to lead students to perceive the teacher as caring about their welfare: empathy, understanding, and responsiveness. Teven and McCroskey's (1997) research provided evidence that perceived caring is associated with increased affective learning and perceived cognitive learning in the classroom. They suggest that the strong relationships between nonverbal immediacy and perceived caring, both of which have been found to have an association with affective learning, suggest that the nonverbal immediacy behaviors of the teacher may be cuing students' perceptions of teacher caring.

Teacher Immediacy and Clarity

Clarity includes such features as expressiveness, message clarity, teacher explanation, structuring, direct instruction, explicit teaching, teacher elaboration, message fidelity, task structuring, coaching, and scaffolding. Most of this work has centered on what the teacher says—specifically, the style factors in the teacher's messages. Teacher clarity has been found to be positively related to student affective learning. Sidelinger and McCroskey (1997) assert that teacher clarity is an important component of teacher effectiveness. Clarity in instruction enhances student cognitive learning, and it also increases student affect for both the instructor and the subject matter. What's more, an instructor who is perceived as clear and understandable by her or his students is also perceived as nonverbally immediate, assertive, and responsive.

Relationships of Teacher Clarity, Immediacy, and Student Anxiety

Both increased clarity and teacher immediacy have been found to decrease student state receiver apprehension. The combination of the two is even more effective in reducing student anxiety (Chesebro & McCroskey, 1998). Given the negative impact of receiver apprehension and learning (see Chapter 11), these research findings are important and offer teachers two ways to facilitate their students' learning by making it less anxiety provoking.

If we revisit the earlier example of a teacher misbehaving, we can see that non-immediate teacher behaviors add to the anxiety that most students feel in reaction to a violation of stated policies. To reduce the students' state anxiety, that teacher used very immediate behaviors and clearly explained the purpose of the exercise to the satisfaction of the students. Certainly, the anxiety in that example was partially reduced by the retraction of the threat, but the use of clarity and immediacy also served to increase students' affect and, hopefully, students' cognitive learning.

Student Perceptions in Intercultural Contexts

McCroskey's (2002) recent intercultural research focusing on perceptions of instructor effectiveness revealed that, with the exception of student ethnocentrism, individual student variables such as willingness to communicate, general motivation, and intercultural communication apprehension do not appear to be meaningful predictors of perceived differences in the effectiveness of domestic and international instructors. Although ethnocentrism accounted for a small amount of variance, factors other than ethnocentrism were responsible for most of the differences observed. It was found that domestic students did rate foreign teachers as somewhat less effective than domestic teachers in the classroom, but the reason for this result remained unclear in McCroskey's first study.

Subsequently, research was conducted to examine perceptions of teacher behaviors (assertiveness and responsiveness, immediacy, and clarity) in conjunction with other variables that could reasonably be assumed to have some predictive value for instructor effectiveness ratings. McCroskey (2003) found in her second study that, once again, U.S. students' domestic instructors were evaluated somewhat more positively than foreign instructors. In addition, the students in this second study, in classes taught by U.S. teachers, reported that they believed the teachers were more effective, that they had higher affect toward the course content and the instructor, and that they perceived lower learning loss.

Because this study was in large part a replication of the previous study, these results were expected. However, it is important that this finding not be overgeneralized. Approximately 30 percent of the students in this study rated their foreign instructor *more positively* than they rated their domestic teacher. Thus, although it is accurate to conclude that many foreign instructors are deemed to be less effective than domestic instructors, it is not correct to conclude that this extends to all foreign instructors. Clearly, customary instructional communication behaviors vary widely among foreign teachers, just as they do among domestic teachers, and some are more effective than others. Moreover, it is not necessarily that students don't like foreign teachers (or domestic teachers, for that matter); it is more that they do not like certain behaviors.

The results of the research suggest that the way to improve the quality of instruction of foreign instructors in the United States is the same as the way to improve the instruction of domestic teachers in the United States: Teach them to employ the kinds of instructional communication behaviors that have been found to be effective in the United States, such as assertiveness, responsiveness, immediacy, and clarity. The results of this research suggest that foreign teachers are effective in the United States *if they engage in these behaviors*, and are not effective if they do not.

In sum, teachers are rated differently based on what they do in the classroom. The qualitative differences between those who behave and those who misbehave are noticed by students, and these differences do have an impact on student learning.

You were promised a list of what you should do to remedy your misbehaviors and enhance your teaching in the classroom. The following recommendations are suggested:

1. Use immediate, clear, and caring behaviors in your classroom.
2. Don't misbehave; but, if you do, offer your students a reasonable explanation, apologize to them, and explain why the misbehavior is atypical—why it does not represent your normally appropriate behavior.
3. Regularly check for student feedback regarding their expectations and perceptions of your behavior.

References

Chesebro, J. L., & McCroskey, J. C. (1998). The relationship of teacher clarity and teacher immediacy with students' experiences of state receiver apprehension. *Communication Quarterly, 46,* 446–456.

Dolin, D. J. (1995). *Ain't misbehavin': A study of teacher misbehaviors, related communication behaviors, and student resistance.* Unpublished doctoral dissertation, West Virginia University, Morgantown.

Kearney, P., Plax, T. G., & Allen, T. H. (2002). Understanding student reactions to teachers who misbehave. In J. L. Chesebro & J. C. McCroskey (Eds.), *Communication for teachers* (pp. 127–140). Boston: Allyn & Bacon.

McCroskey, L. L. (2002). Domestic and international college instructors: An examination of perceived differences and their correlates. *Journal of Intercultural Communication Research, 31*(2), 63–84.

McCroskey, L. L. (2003). Relationships of instructional communication styles of domestic and foreign instructors with instructional outcomes. *Journal of Intercultural Communication Research, 32*(2), 75–96.

Sidelinger, R. J., & McCroskey, J. C. (1997). Communication correlates of teacher clarity in the college classroom. *Communication Research Reports, 14,* 1–10.

Teven, J. J., & McCroskey, J. C. (1997). The relationship of perceived teacher caring with student learning and teacher evaluation. *Communication Education, 46,* 1–9.

Thweatt, K. S., & McCroskey, J. C. (1996). Teacher nonimmediacy and misbehavior: Unintentional negative communication. *Communication Research Reports, 13*(2), 198–204.

Thweatt, K. S., & McCroskey, J. C. (1998). The impact of teacher immediacy and misbehaviors on teacher credibility. *Communication Education, 47,* 348–358.

Glossary

ethnocentrism   The tendency of people to see their culture as the central (and most valid) culture in the world and to evaluate the behavior of people from other cultures by the standards of their own culture.

incompetent teacher behaviors   Teacher behaviors that indicate that the teacher is not well informed on the subject matter or on appropriate instructional practices.

indolent teacher behaviors   Teacher behaviors that are discourteous to students, such as missing class, arriving late, engaging in delinquent grading, forgetting polices or promises to the students, or ignoring student needs.

offensive teacher behaviors   Teacher behaviors that are rude, humiliating, condescending, or cruel to students.

teacher misbehavior   Any teacher behavior that interferes with the learning of students or that violates reasonable expectations of students.

14

Nonverbal Communication in the Classroom

The previous 13 chapters of this book have been devoted primarily to verbal communication. This last chapter is devoted to nonverbal communication. This 13:1 ratio may be seen by many as quite appropriate, for they see nonverbal communication to be comparatively unimportant. They might question whether even a single chapter should be devoted to such "trivial" matters.

As you might surmise, given the title of this chapter, we do not share the view that nonverbal communication is unimportant. In fact, we believe that nonverbal behavior may be even more important in human communication than verbal behavior. As we explain in our book on this topic (Richmond & McCroskey, 2004), this is probably true in many contexts. The classroom context is definitely a case in point.

Nonverbal communication is *the process of one person stimulating meaning in the mind of another person (or persons) by means of nonverbal messages*. Although some people would prefer to define nonverbal communication as "communication without words," this is misleading. Nonverbal messages are often sent and received by people who exchange no words, but words are seldom exchanged by people in the absence of nonverbal messages. Thus, it is normal for both verbal and nonverbal messages to be exchanged simultaneously.

People who prefer the "without words" definition may be confusing words with "language." Indeed, that which is a message, but is not a language code, is nonverbal. Thus, gestures that substitute for words (emblems) and American Sign Language (the gestural language of the deaf) should be considered verbal communication, because they represent coded equivalents of words. This is also the case with drum languages, Morse code, smoke signals, and so on. All of these linguistic systems use word substitutes and, therefore, are verbal in nature. A few other distinctions will help us understand why it is so important to study nonverbal communication in the classroom.

Nonverbal/Verbal Distinctions

Three distinctions between nonverbal and verbal communication are particularly useful when considering classroom communication. They are content versus relational goals, cognitive versus affective impacts, and intentional versus unintentional behaviors. Let us consider each.

Content versus Relational Goals

Verbal messages are sent in classrooms with the primary goal of communicating subject-matter content. When teachers carefully prepare for class, they are most concerned with the selection and organization of the content, whether they can make ideas clear, and whether the students will understand. By contrast, nonverbal messages are more commonly sent to establish relationships. The nonverbal message says how the teacher feels about both the content and the student. It should be recognized, however, that this is not an absolute distinction. Both have impact in the other's domain as well as their own.

Cognitive versus Affective Impact

Verbal messages have their primary impact on cognitive responses, or how the student thinks about the subject-matter content. Nonverbal messages, by contrast, have their primary impact on affective responses—how the student feels about both the subject matter and the teacher. However, both have impact in the other's area as well. It is possible to achieve cognitive success (the student learns the lesson content) while simultaneously having affective failure (the student hates that content and/or dislikes the teacher), or the opposite.

Intentional versus Unintentional Behavior

The overwhelming majority of our verbal messages are, or at least have the strong potential to be, under our conscious control. Since there are so many nonverbal messages being given off simultaneously and constantly, we are not consciously aware of most of them. We can, however, be more effective teachers to the extent that we bring more of our nonverbal messages under our conscious control.

To summarize, verbal messages in the classroom typically are intentionally used to help the student gain cognitive control over the subject-matter content. Nonverbal behaviors, in contrast, are usually unintentionally sent as messages that have positive or negative affective impact on the student, with resulting positive or negative relationships being built between the student and the content as well as between the student and the teacher. As we have stressed throughout this book, these affective relationships often are as important as, or even more important than, the cognitive mastery that the student may achieve.

Nonverbal Message Categories

Although many nonverbal behaviors occur simultaneously, it is helpful to look at individual categories of such behaviors. When these behaviors are controlled and performed with the intention of sending a message, they generally are called nonverbal "codes," because they represent encoded messages. Students, of course, seldom can be sure whether what they observe teachers doing represents uncontrolled behaviors or controlled codes, so they tend to treat them both alike. We will consider seven categories here: eye behavior, space, touch, body movement and gesture, voice, time, and environment.

[handwritten margin note: when nonverbal messages are controlled they are called nv "codes" b/c they represent encoded messages]

Eye Behavior

It is said that the "eyes are the mirror of the soul." Although that may be more poetic than accurate, people do look at a person's eyes when they are trying to understand and interpret what that person is saying. There are three types of eye behavior that may be of concern in the classroom: eye contact, staring, and pupil dilation.

1. *Eye contact.* When people look directly into one another's eyes, we say they have made eye contact. Such contact bridges distances between people and makes them feel closer. Eye contact establishes psychological contact between two people, but it can become threatening if held too long. Effective teachers regularly establish eye contact with their students. This holds attention and permits the student to signal confusion or understanding. It signals that the teacher cares about the student and, if not held too long, is perceived positively by most students. When teachers lecture to students without establishing eye contact, as often happens in high school and college classrooms, students tend to lose interest and feel the course has nothing to do with them personally. They may believe that the teacher does not care whether they learn or not, which often accurately represents the teacher's real views.

2. *Staring.* Staring is continuous looking by one person directed toward another. It may or may not involve eye contact, depending on the situation. Teachers often use the "teacher stare" for disciplinary reasons. We all can think back to that time we were not paying attention and then became aware the teacher was staring at us. Such staring is a control technique that is certainly superior to stopping the class and yelling at a student. However, teachers should be aware that students generally will look where the teacher is looking if they stare too long. That includes staring out the window!

3. *Pupil dilation.* The pupil of the eye involuntarily responds to light and darkness differentially, becoming smaller in bright light and larger when the lights are dim. Although most people are unaware of it, the pupils also tend to dilate (become larger) when people look at something that interests or arouses them. Seasoned poker players use this involuntary response to learn whether their opponent has a good hand. They also wear glasses or hats that shade their eyes so that others will

not be able to read the dilation of their own eyes. Astute teachers can tell when their students are interested by looking at the level of dilation in their eyes. This method, of course, may be limited by class size or by lighting that is either very bright or very dim.

Space

If you want to find out how powerfully use of space can communicate, the next time you get into an elevator alone with a stranger, intentionally stand right next to her or him. But be careful—you may get a surprisingly strong message in response. If you are bit less venturesome, try getting into a crowded elevator and standing with your back to the door while looking at the other people. Most of them will become a bit uncomfortable. They may tell you to turn around, or ask you what you are staring at. Some are likely to escape on the first floor at which the elevator stops.

Spatial messages can have a strong impact in the classroom, sometimes a very negative one. To understand why students react to space the ways they do, it is helpful to look at space from two different vantage points: territoriality and personal space.

1. *Territoriality.* Territoriality is a basic animal instinct. Dogs, bears, and other animals identify a territory that they consider to be their own and protect it from intrusions by other animals. Some animals, such as dogs, mark their territory by urinating at its boundaries. Other dogs come near, smell the other dog's odor, and veer away. If they cross that line, however, the owner dog is very likely to attack the intruder. Sometimes this leads to a fight to the death.

Humans have the same basic territorial instinct as dogs do, although most of us do not identify our territory in the same way! We do, however, react almost as strongly if somebody dares to mess with what is ours. The biggest cause of student misbehavior in the lower grades comes from one child infringing on another's "turf" and the owner coming to the defense of what he or she believes to be her or his territory.

Teachers need to recognize the cause of such problems and avoid excessive punishment of instinctive behavior. Such behavior is very difficult to control. When children understand it better, they are more likely to be able to restrain the instinct. But full-grown, well-educated adults may behave the same way—even teachers!

The teacher's desk is the teacher's territory, and woe be it to the unfortunate child who invades it. Normally calm, controlled teachers are apt to go into a rage if their desk is invaded. Yet some of these same teachers will think nothing of invading their students' desks or lockers. Totally innocent students may react instinctually and may deeply resent the teacher's behavior. A positive teacher–student relationship that has taken months, even years, to develop may be destroyed in moments.

Invading another person's space communicates a powerful nonverbal message. It says "I do not respect you, so I do not respect your territory." When students recognize that sitting at another person's desk will get that person upset, many will not do it anymore. However, bullies will do it even more than before. It is important that the invader, not the invaded, be punished for the ensuing confrontation.

2. *Personal space.* One's personal space is much like one's territory. The difference is that territory is relatively fixed, whereas one's personal space moves wherever the person goes. If you travel to the opposite side of the world, your territory stays at home, but your personal space travels with you.

An individual's personal space is an "invisible bubble" surrounding that person. Only people with whom one has an intimate relationship are generally allowed within the bubble. The bubble is adjusted to fit the available space. If one gets into a crowded elevator, the bubble will shrink to a very small size. If one is walking in the open countryside, it may expand to giant proportions.

We treat our personal space much as we do our territory. If someone invades it, we may become very upset. When someone stands too close or moves into our immediate area, we may take steps to protect ourselves from the intruder.

Young children, of course, are very insensitive to both territoriality and personal space. They are little "space invaders." Their "invasions" can be very disturbing to new teachers who have not been prepared to accept behavior that, at least for adults, is very unusual. As children get older, however, it is increasingly likely that the teacher will be the invader. Teachers often exert their power by invading the space of their students, sometimes without realizing they are doing so. If students react negatively, the teacher seldom sees her- or himself as the cause of the problem. More likely, he or she will believe that the student has something to hide or is just a surly individual. Sometimes teachers even go so far as to punish the student for reacting to the teacher's own invasion. Naturally, such behavior will have an extremely negative impact on the teacher's relationship with that student.

Touch

One wag has defined touch as "zero space." Although touch is much more than that, that is certainly part of what it is. We cannot understand the impact of touch as a nonverbal message without understanding space. Touch is the ultimate invasion of one's personal space—the total elimination of the invisible bubble. We don't let just anybody touch us, for our personal space is sacred to us.

The general culture of the United States is one of the most nontouching cultures in the world. As descendants of the Puritans, people in this culture tend to associate touch with sex, and since in the puritanical framework sex is bad, touch must also be bad. Any touching involving much more than a handshake between people of the same sex, particularly males, is viewed as an indication of homosexual tendencies. Touch by opposite-sex couples is viewed with only slightly more acceptance, unless the two are married and the touch is not open to public view. While many people in American society do not fully accept these cultural norms, most adapt to them for fear of retribution from those who do. They are wise to do so, for court interpretations of laws against sexual harassment have gone so far as to declare even looking at the body of another person— much less touching it— to be illegal in some cases!

Although people in many other cultures around the world laugh at what they consider our amusingly quaint touch norms, touch is far and away the most intimate form of communication for Americans. Touching or holding a person who is grieving can communicate our sympathy far better than any words we might use. By contrast, a touch that is seen as inappropriate may set off such a confrontation that hundreds of passersby on a street will stop to observe. Touch is, indeed, our most potent communicative message.

Touch can be useful in the classroom, at least in the lower grades. It may be used to comfort or control a small child or to express affection and caring. It is virtually impossible to imagine a kindergarten where teachers do not touch the children. Nevertheless, teachers must be very careful with messages of touch. They must recognize that some parents are so extremely touch avoidant, they make Puritans look like public gropers! Such parents teach their children that all touching is bad and that people who touch them are bad people. Although this is almost always done with the best of intentions—specifically, to protect the children from being sexually molested—young children are often unable to distinguish between "good touch" and "bad touch."

Many teachers, even those who work with very young children, have had their careers and lives ruined by false allegations of molestation. It is important for the teacher to realize that such an allegation will be accepted as true by a large proportion of the public, even if it is never proven and even if a court finds the teacher not guilty of any misbehavior. A person accused of sexual molestation or sexual harassment is presumed guilty in this society until proven innocent. And it is impossible to prove that such a behavior never occurred. The best advice for teachers, therefore, is *don't touch*. The benefits of touch to the child, though potentially large, can never outweigh the potential harms to the teacher, which are catastrophic.

Body Movement and Gesture

People look at other people in their environment in an attempt to figure out what they are like. When people talk, they look even more intently at each other, believing that the way a person uses her or his body will help one to understand what he or she is saying. This general pattern applies in the classroom as well.

Movement is an attention getter. Things that are moving are generally more interesting than things that are stationary. When a teacher moves while teaching, student attention will typically follow the teacher. In general, teachers who remain stationary, whether standing or sitting, are seen as more boring than teachers who move.

Movement can also be used as a communicative message. When a student speaks softly, the tendency of many teachers is to move toward the student to hear better or to ask the student to speak up. The former behavior is actually likely to cause the student to speak even more softly, while the latter is likely to embarrass the student and decrease the likelihood that he or she will participate in the future.

In contrast, moving back, away from the student, while maintaining constant eye contact, is most likely to communicate the need to speak louder and result in the desired behavior on the part of the student.

Gestures may be particularly helpful to the teacher. We use gestures to describe and clarify things and to regulate the flow of communication in the classroom. We point to students when it is their turn to speak, we have students raise their hands to be heard, and so on. One type of gestures, called adaptors, occur when students are tense or nervous, particularly during testing. These gestures include rubbing oneself, playing with one's hair, toying with a pencil, shaking a leg, and so on. Teachers should recognize the cause of these behaviors and try to reduce the tension in the room if possible.

Voice

With every spoken word comes a nonverbal vocal message. Our vocal tones communicate our feelings. They tell the listener how to interpret the words or groups of words we say.

Our voices also tell people about who we are. All people speak with an accent; there is no such thing as unaccented spoken language. Hence, when we talk, we tell people where we come from. Research also indicates that with only the information provided by the voice, listeners can draw an incredible number of perceptions about the speaker. These include such demographic factors as sex, age, region of origin, educational level, and occupation. But listeners can also perceive all manner of personality variations based only on these vocal cues. Some of these perceptions are likely to be correct, but many will be incorrect. Thus, it is important that the teacher know what kind of perceptions her or his voice generates so that these can be corrected if necessary.

Research on teachers' communication in the classroom indicates that the single most negative nonverbal communication behavior a teacher can perform is to speak with a lack of vocal variety. Monotonous speaking voices put students to sleep. Some will actually fall asleep. Others will stay physically awake, but their minds will be diverted to something more interesting. Vocal variety is critical to maintaining students' interest and attention. Even adult learners cannot maintain attention toward a monotonous speaker more than a short time.

Time

The way people use time communicates strongly to others. We can impress or offend by our use of time. Every culture has particular ways of using and treating time. In the general American culture, we distinguish between formal and informal time. Formal time is "clock" time. Informal time is expressed in the English language in many ways—"in a while," "before long," "after a bit," "forever," "never," "in a minute," "tomorrow," "this afternoon"—and all of these expressions must be learned by children in the culture.

Nearly everyone has had (or will have) the opportunity to travel with a child who has not learned formal time yet. "When will we get there?" and "Are we there yet?" can become very tiring, but they are of genuine concern to children. One of the first things we begin working on with children in school is to teach them formal time. Usually, it takes quite a while for children to master the system, but eventually they do.

Nothing about time seems to be inborn, not even the concepts of past, present, and future. However, one aspect of time usage comes about as close to being inborn as you can get: an orientation toward time and activity. Some people are morning people, and others are night people. It is difficult at best, and often impossible, to change a person from one to the other. Morning people are up at the crack of dawn and take the view that "the early bird catches the worm." Night people wish the morning people would be quiet and let them sleep. They are certain such people deserve the worms and are quite willing to let them have them. Night people start functioning in the late morning or early afternoon. They reach their peak in the evening, when the morning people are having trouble keeping their eyes open. They encourage these "party poopers" to go to bed—no one will miss them. But the morning people wish the "night crawlers" would just be quiet so they could sleep. It is as if there were one world inhabited by two distinct species that are totally incompatible.

Although some people are not clear members of either species, if you are one or the other, you know it, and you probably look at the other group with more than mild disdain. This would be an amusing battle with no implications for teachers at all, except that the two species had a war over who would control education in this culture, and the morning people won.

They have not proven to be good winners. They have chosen to enslave the night people. They force them to get up before dawn throughout most of the winter and then ride a bus to school, listening to screaming morning children all the way, before they are even awake. The night children who are unfortunate enough to have morning parents may even have food forced down their throats before they get on the bus. The bouncing bus can be enough to make them regurgitate the unwanted repast. Nevertheless, they usually survive until lunchtime and begin waking up. They have another hour or two while they are awake enough to learn something, but by now the morning people are getting tired, so only the unimportant subjects are taught at this point. Then, just when the day is getting going, the night children are thrown out of school, placed on buses, and sent home—where, of course, they will be told to go to bed hours before they are ready to go to sleep.

Not until college are these children allowed to learn at a time that is good for them. They now regale their struggling morning enemies with glorious tales of the wonders of late-night television. They enjoy laughing at the morning "nerds" who are so out of it. You see, there was another war. This one was for the colleges and universities, and the night people won. But they did not choose to have all classes meet in the afternoon and at night, as much as the morning people feared they would. (It's not that they are better winners than the morning people, but that, when they are wide awake, they would rather party than study anyhow!)

Although this description may be a bit of a flight of fancy, written by an author who is happy to be finishing one of the last chapters of a book, the exaggeration of the tale may make the point better than a more direct rendition. Elementary and secondary schools really are dominated by people whose time/activity orientations are on the extreme morning side. Colleges really are populated by large groups of students who absolutely reject that orientation and who are willing to reject learning if necessary.

What goes unnoticed in all of this are the many, many children who are night people struggling but failing to adapt to the morning orientation of the schools. This time orientation sends a strong message to those children that they are not bright, they are lazy, and they cannot learn. Those who reach college learn that the message was false, but many never get that far.

While no single teacher can overcome the problems this system may cause, those teaching intact classes at the elementary level can make a real difference in their own classes. All they need to do is vary the time at which the individual subjects are taught so that no subject is always taught first thing in the morning or right after lunch. This will tend to equalize the opportunities to learn for the children who do not function well early.

Environment

The characteristics of an environment, such as a classroom, and the objects in it have a powerful impact on the communication that occurs within that environment. The messages produced by the environment merge with other verbal and nonverbal messages to color all the meanings that are stimulated.

To start with, the very attractiveness of the learning environment itself communicates the value of education to the student. If it is old and dirty, the student associates what is taught with that appearance and devalues what is presented. Research has consistently indicated that both children and adults resent being placed in unattractive surroundings. They will do their best to get out of those surroundings. They will also develop negative attitudes toward other people and ideas they encounter in those surroundings. Teachers like students less, students like teachers less, and students devalue what they are being taught. Within reason, money and effort spent to enhance the attractiveness of the teaching/learning environment is money well spent.

Many things can be done to enhance an environment that do not take enormous amounts of either time or money. For example, choosing pastel colors when rooms are being painted does not cost more but will create a better learning climate than choosing colors that are too bright (like red and orange), which overexcite the students, or too dull (like dark brown and several shades of green), which will depress everyone in the room. Keeping a good temperature for learning (68 to 72 degrees is recommended) may actually save money, for many schools and classrooms are much too warm for learning. Lighting should be bright enough for students to see well everywhere in the room, but glare should be avoided, because it raises both stress and exhaustion levels. Natural lighting, since it is so hard to control, is more problematic than artificial lighting, which can be held constant. In particular, eye-level windows should be avoided if possible, covered if not. Such windows were vital in schools a century ago, because artificial lighting was not satisfactory. Today, such windows serve primarily to distract students and teacher alike.

However the environment is controlled, it is important that the students feel it is "their" environment. Particularly for schools that have intact classes, as is common at the elementary level, it is critical that the students have a feeling of ownership. This will help make the children feel secure and important. The child should refer to the room as "my" classroom, not "Mr. or Ms. So-and-So's" classroom. To accomplish this, teacher-centered objects should be kept to a minimum. Some teachers intentionally take possession of the room by decorating everything and bringing in many objects from home. Although this may make the teacher feel more comfortable, it may make students feel like unwelcome outsiders. Children should be allowed and encouraged (but never forced) to work together to decorate bulletin boards and other areas of the room. This means that the children's work that is displayed should be selected by the children, not by the teacher. Sometimes work that a teacher thinks is great is embarrassing to the child who did it.

In conclusion, there are many nonverbal factors that affect the teaching/ learning process. In this chapter, we have only skimmed the surface of the nonverbal arena. Teachers who are conscious of their own use of nonverbal communication are almost always better teachers than those who are not.

References

Richmond, V. P. (1997). *Nonverbal communication in the classroom,* 2nd ed. Acton, MA: Tapestry Press.

Richmond, V. P., & McCroskey, J. C. (2004). *Nonverbal behavior in interpersonal relations,* 5th ed. Boston: Allyn & Bacon.

Glossary

chronemics   The study of the impact of time in communication.

environment   The natural and human-controlled elements surrounding all communication events.

haptics   The study of touch and the ways it is used to communicate. In the U.S. culture, this is the most potent form of nonverbal communication.

kinesics   The study of body movement and gesture.

nonverbal communication   The process of one person stimulating meaning in the mind of another person (or persons) by means of nonverbal messages.

oculesics   The study of eye behavior, eye contact, eye movement, and the functions of eye behavior.

personal space   An invisible bubble (of space) that surrounds an individual and expands and contracts as a function of culture, personality, and relationships with others.

proxemics   The study of the ways in which humans use and communicate with space.

territoriality   An instinct shared by humans and other species to identify, occupy, and protect what they perceive to be their territory.

verbal communication   The process of one person stimulating meaning in the mind of another person (or persons) through linguistic messages, which may be either oral or written.

vocalics   The study of the use of vocal behavior in communication.

Teacher and Trainer Communication Traits

This appendix provides five measures that teachers and trainers may use to self-diagnose potential assets or problems related to their own trait orientations toward communication. These include the instruments designed to measure Willingness to Communicate, Communication Apprehension, Shyness, Self-Perceived Communication Competence, and Compulsive Communication.

These measures may also be used to identify students who may have problems with communication. The students should be provided only with the directions and the scale items. The remaining information here is for teachers and trainers only. Obviously, younger children cannot complete these scales. Teachers will need to determine whether children in their upper-grade classes can do so. In most cases, these scales can be used with students in classes above the fifth-grade level.

Willingness to Communicate (WTC)

Directions: Below are 20 situations in which a person might choose to communicate or not to communicate. Presume you have completely free choice. Indicate the percentage of times you would choose to communicate in each type of situation. Indicate in the space at the left of the item what percent of the time you would choose to communicate (0 = Never to 100 = Always).

_____ 1. Talk with a service station attendant.
_____ 2. Talk with a physician.
_____ 3. Present a talk to a group of strangers.
_____ 4. Talk with an acquaintance while standing in line.
_____ 5. Talk with a salesperson in a store.
_____ 6. Talk in a large meeting of friends.

_____ 7. Talk with a police officer.

_____ 8. Talk in a small group of strangers.

_____ 9. Talk with a friend while standing in line.

_____ 10. Talk with a waiter/waitress in a restaurant.

_____ 11. Talk in a large meeting of acquaintances.

_____ 12. Talk with a stranger while standing in line.

_____ 13. Talk with a secretary.

_____ 14. Present a talk to a group of friends.

_____ 15. Talk in a small group of acquaintances.

_____ 16. Talk with a garbage collector.

_____ 17. Talk in a large meeting of strangers.

_____ 18. Talk with a spouse (or girl/boyfriend).

_____ 19. Talk in a small group of friends.

_____ 20. Present a talk to a group of acquaintances.

Scoring:

Context-type subscores:

Group Discussion: Add scores for items 8, 15, 19; then divide by 3.

Meetings: Add scores for items 6, 11, 17; then divide by 3.

Interpersonal: Add scores for items 4, 9, 12; then divide by 3.

Public Speaking: Add scores for items 3, 14, 20; then divide by 3.

Receiver-type subscores:

Stranger: Add scores for items 3, 8, 12, 17; then divide by 4.

Acquaintance: Add scores for items 4, 11, 15, 20; then divide by 4.

Friend: Add scores for items 6, 9, 14, 19; then divide by 4.

To compute the total WTC score, add the subscores for stranger, acquaintance, and friend. Then divide by 3. All scores, total and subscores, will fall in the range of 0 to 100

Norms for WTC Scores:

Group Discussion: >89 High WTC, <57 Low WTC

Meetings: >80 High WTC, <39 Low WTC

Interpersonal Conversations: >94 High WTC, <64 Low WTC

Public Speaking: >78 High WTC, <33 Low WTC

Stranger: >63 High WTC, <18 Low WTC

Acquaintance: >92 High WTC, <57 Low WTC

Friend: >99 High WTC, <71 Low WTC

Total WTC: >82 High Overall WTC, <52 Low Overall WTC

Sources:

McCroskey, J. C. (1992). Reliability and validity of the willingness to communicate scale. *Communication Quarterly, 40,* 16–25.

McCroskey, J. C., & Richmond, V. P. (1987). Willingness to communicate. In J. C. McCroskey & J. A. Daly (Eds.), *Personality and interpersonal communication* (pp. 119–131). Newbury Park, CA: Sage.

Personal Report of Communication Apprehension (PRCA-24)

Directions: This instrument is composed of 24 statements concerning feelings about communicating with others. Please indicate the degree to which each statement applies to you by marking whether you: **Strongly Disagree = 1; Disagree = 2; Are Neutral = 3; Agree = 4; Strongly Disagree = 5.**

_____ 1. I dislike participating in group discussions.

_____ 2. Generally, I am comfortable while participating in group discussions.

_____ 3. I am tense and nervous while participating in group discussions.

_____ 4. I like to get involved in group discussions.

_____ 5. Engaging in a group discussion with new people makes me tense and nervous.

_____ 6. I am calm and relaxed while participating in group discussions.

_____ 7. Generally, I am nervous when I have to participate in a meeting.

_____ 8. Usually, I am comfortable when I have to participate in a meeting.

_____ 9. I am very calm and relaxed when I am called upon to express an opinion at a meeting.

_____ 10. I am afraid to express myself at meetings.

_____ 11. Communicating at meetings usually makes me uncomfortable.

_____ 12. I am very relaxed when answering questions at a meeting.

_____ 13. While participating in a conversation with a new acquaintance, I feel very nervous.

_____ 14. I have no fear of speaking up in conversations.

_____ 15. Ordinarily I am very tense and nervous in conversations.

_____ 16. Ordinarily I am very calm and relaxed in conversations.

_____ 17. While conversing with a new acquaintance, I feel very relaxed.

_____ 18. I'm afraid to speak up in conversations.

_____ 19. I have no fear of giving a speech.

_____ 20. Certain parts of my body feel very tense and rigid while giving a speech.

_____ 21. I feel relaxed while giving a speech.

_____ 22. My thoughts become confused and jumbled when I am giving a speech.

_____ 23. I face the prospect of giving a speech with confidence.

_____ 24. While giving a speech, I get so nervous I forget facts I really know.

Scoring:
Group Discussion: 18 + (scores for items 2, 4, 6) − (scores for items 1,3, 5)
Meetings: 18 + (scores for items 8, 9, 12) − (scores for items 7, 10, 11)
Interpersonal: 18 + (scores for items 14, 16, 17) − (scores for items 13, 15, 18)
Public Speaking: 18 + (scores for items 19, 21, 23) − (scores for items 20, 22, 24)

Group Discussion Score: _____
Meetings Score: _____
Interpersonal Score: _____
Public Speaking Score: _____

To obtain your total score for the PRCA, add your subscores together. _____

Interpretation: Scores can range from 24 to 120. Scores below 51 represent people who have very low CA. Scores between 51 and 80 represent people with average CA. Scores above 80 represent people who have high levels of trait CA.

Norms for the PRCA-24:

(Based on over 40,000 college students; data from over 3,000 nonstudent adults in a national sample provided virtually identical norms, within 0.20 for all scores.)

	Mean	*Standard Deviation*	*High*	*Low*
Total Score	65.6	15.3	> 80	< 51
Group:	15.4	4.8	> 20	< 11
Meeting:	16.4	4.2	> 20	< 13
Dyad (Interpersonal):	14.2	3.9	> 18	< 11
Public:	19.3	5.1	> 24	< 14

Source: McCroskey, J. C. (1982). *An introduction to rhetorical communication,* 4th ed. Englewood Cliffs, NJ: Prentice Hall.
      (Also available in more recent editions of this book, now published by Allyn & Bacon.)

McCroskey Shyness Scale (SS)

Directions: Below are fourteen statements that people sometimes make about themselves. Please indicate whether or not you believe each statement applies to you by marking whether you: **Strongly Disagree = 1; Disagree = 2; Neutral = 3; Agree = 4; Strongly Agree = 5.**

_____ 1. I am a shy person.

_____ 2. Other people think I talk a lot.

_____ 3. I am a very talkative person.

_____ 4. Other people think I am shy.

_____ 5. I talk a lot.

_____ 6. I tend to be very quiet in class.

_____ 7. I don't talk much.

_____ 8. I talk more than most people.

_____ 9. I am a quiet person.

_____10. I talk more in a small group (3–6) than others do.

_____11. Most people talk more than I do.

_____12. Other people think I am very quiet.

_____13. I talk more in class than most people do.

_____14. Most people are more shy than I am.

Scoring:
Step 1. Add the scores for items 1, 4, 6, 7, 9, 11, and 12.
Step 2. Add the scores for items 2, 3, 5, 8, 10, 13, and 14.
Step 3. Complete the formula: Shyness = 42 + Total of Step 2 – Total of Step 1.

Interpretation: Scores may range between 14 and 70. Scores above 52 indicate a high level of shyness. Scores below 32 indicate a low level of shyness. Scores between 32 and 52 indicate a moderate level of shyness.

Source: McCroskey, J. C., & Richmond, V. P. (1982). Communication apprehension and shyness: Conceptual and operational distinctions. *Central States Speech Journal, 33,* 458–468.

Self-Perceived Communication Competence Scale (SPCC)

Directions: Below are twelve situations in which you might need to communicate. People's abilities to communicate effectively vary a lot, and sometimes the same person is more competent to communicate in one situation than in another. Please indicate how competent you believe you are to communicate in each of the situations described below. Indicate in the space provided at the left of each item your estimate of your competence.

Presume 0 = completely incompetent and 100 = competent.

_____ 1. Present a talk to a group of strangers.

_____ 2. Talk with an acquaintance.

_____ 3. Talk in a large meeting of friends.

_____ 4. Talk in a small group of strangers.

_____ 5. Talk with a friend.

_____ 6. Talk in a large meeting of acquaintances.

_____ 7. Talk with a stranger.

_____ 8. Present a talk to a group of friends.

_____ 9. Talk in a small group of acquaintances.

_____ 10. Talk in a large meeting of strangers.

_____ 11. Talk in a small group of friends.

_____ 12. Present a talk to a group of acquaintances.

Scoring: To compute the subscores, add the percentages for the items indicated and divide the total by the number indicated below.

Public = 1 + 8 + 12; divide by 3.
Meeting = 3 + 6 + 10; divide by 3.
Group = 4 + 9 + 11; divide by 3.
Dyad = 2 + 5 + 7; divide by 3.
Stranger = 1 + 4 + 7 + 10; divide by 4.
Acquaintance = 2 + 6 + 9 + 12; divide by 4.
Friend = 3 + 5 + 8 + 11; divide by 4.

To compute the total SPCC score, add the subscores for Stranger, Acquaintance, and Friend. Then, divide that total by 3.

Interpretation:
Public Speaking scores above 86 indicate high competence, below 51 indicate low competence, and 51–86 indicate moderate competence.
Meeting scores above 85 indicate high competence, below 51 indicate low competence, and 51–85 indicate moderate competence.
Group scores above 90 indicate high competence, below 61 indicate low competence, and 61–90 indicate moderate competence.
Dyad scores above 93 indicate high competence, below 68 indicate low competence, and 68–93 indicate moderate competence.
Stranger scores above 79 indicate high competence, below 31 indicate low competence, and 31–79 indicate moderate competence.
Acquaintance scores above 92 indicate high competence, below 62 indicate low competence, and 62–92 indicate moderate competence.
Friend scores above 98 indicate high competence, below 76 indicate low competence, and 76–98 indicate moderate competence.
Total scores above 87 indicate high competence, below 59 indicate low competence, and 59–87 indicate moderate competence.

Source: McCroskey, J. C., & McCroskey, L. L. (1988). Self-report as an approach to measuring communication competence. *Communication Research Reports, 5,* 108–113.

Talkaholic Scale

Directions: Read the following questions and select the answer that corresponds with what you would do in most situations. Do not be concerned if some of the items appear similar. Please use the scale below to rate the degree to which each statement applies to you. Use the following responses: **Strongly Disagree = 1; Disagree = 2; Neutral = 3; Agree = 4; Strongly Agree = 5.**

_____ 1. Often I keep quiet when I should talk.

_____ 2. I talk more than I should sometimes.

_____ 3. Often, I talk when I know I should keep quiet.

_____ 4. Sometimes I keep quiet when I know it would be to my advantage to talk.

_____ 5. I am a "talkaholic."

_____ 6. Sometimes I feel compelled to keep quiet.

_____ 7. In general, I talk more than I should.

_____ 8. I am a compulsive talker.

_____ 9. I am not a talker; rarely do I talk in communication situations.

_____10. Quite a few people have said I talk too much.

_____11. I just can't stop talking too much.

_____12. In general, I talk less than I should.

_____13. I am not a "talkaholic."

_____14. Sometimes I talk when I know it would be to my advantage to keep quiet.

_____15. I talk less than I should sometimes.

_____16. I am not a compulsive talker.

Scoring: To determine the score on the Talkaholic Scale, complete the following steps:
Step 1: Add scores for item 2, 3, 5, 7, 8, 10, 11, and 14.
Step 2: Add the scores for items 13 and 16.
Step 3: Complete the following formula: Total Score = 12 + Total from Step 1 − Total from Step 2.

Note: Items 1, 4, 6, 9, 12, and 15 are filler items and are not scored.

Scores may range between 10 and 50. Most people score below 30.

People who score between 30 and 39 are borderline talkaholics, and are able to control their talking most of the time, but sometimes they find themselves in situations where it is difficult to be quiet, even if it would be very much to their advantage not to talk.

People with scores above 40 are talkaholics. They are truly compulsive communicators.

The talkaholic scale is a measure of compulsive communication. Some people are driven to talk. They are highly verbal people and have great difficulty (and often little desire) being quiet in the presence of other people. While these individuals are "high talkers" or "talkaholics," they usually are not the people that others refer to as one who "talks too much." The term "talks too much" usually is applied to people who are saying things another person doesn't want them to say, or they are ineffective communicators. While the term appears to be a quantitative description, it actually is a qualitative reference. Considerable research has determined that the more a person talks (in most cases, unless the person is an incompetent communicator or saying things that are offensive to others), the more positively that person is evaluated by others. They are more likely to be seen as a leader, as being more competent, and more positively on a variety of other person perception variables.

Sources:

McCroskey, J. C., & Richmond, V. P. (1993). Identifying compulsive communicators: The talkaholic scale. *Communication Research Reports, 11,* 39–52.
McCroskey, J. C., & Richmond, V. P. (1995). Correlates of compulsive communication: Quantitative and qualitative characteristics. *Communication Quarterly, 43,* 39–52.

Appendix B

Student Perceptions of Teachers and Trainers

This appendix provides measures that teachers and trainers may use to determine how their students perceive them as teachers. These include the instruments designed to measure the more general concepts of source credibility and task attraction, as well as the instruments that measure perceptions of teacher communication behavior—teacher clarity, teacher immediacy, teacher assertiveness, and teacher responsiveness.

In most cases, these measures can be used with students above the fifth-grade level. However, teachers will need to determine whether they can be used with any given class. The students should be provided only with the directions and the scale items; the remaining information here is for teachers and trainers only.

Source Credibility Measures

Directions: On the scales below, indicate your feelings about "Your Teacher." Numbers 1 and 7 indicate a very strong feeling. Numbers 2 and 6 indicate a strong feeling. Numbers 3 and 5 indicate a fairly weak feeling. Number 4 indicates you are undecided.

1)*	Intelligent	1	2	3	4	5	6	7	Unintelligent
2)	Untrained	1	2	3	4	5	6	7	Trained
3)*	Cares about me	1	2	3	4	5	6	7	Doesn't care about me
4)*	Honest	1	2	3	4	5	6	7	Dishonest
5)*	Has my interests at heart	1	2	3	4	5	6	7	Doesn't have my interests at heart
6)	Untrustworthy	1	2	3	4	5	6	7	Trustworthy
7)	Inexpert	1	2	3	4	5	6	7	Expert

8)	Self-centered	1	2	3	4	5	6	7	Not self-centered
9)*	Concerned with me	1	2	3	4	5	6	7	Not concerned with me
10)*	Honorable	1	2	3	4	5	6	7	Dishonorable
11)*	Informed	1	2	3	4	5	6	7	Uninformed
12)*	Moral	1	2	3	4	5	6	7	Immoral
13)	Incompetent	1	2	3	4	5	6	7	Competent
14)	Unethical	1	2	3	4	5	6	7	Ethical
15)	Insensitive	1	2	3	4	5	6	7	Sensitive
16)*	Bright	1	2	3	4	5	6	7	Stupid
17)	Phony	1	2	3	4	5	6	7	Genuine
18)	Not understanding	1	2	3	4	5	6	7	Understanding

Scoring: To compute the scores, add scores for each item as indicated below: Rescore items with an * with the following format: $1 = 7$; $2 = 6$; $3 = 5$; $4 = 4$; $5 = 3$; $6 = 2$; $7 = 1$.

> *Competence Factor* (add scores for items 1, 2, 7, 11, 13, and 16)_____
> *Caring/Goodwill Factor* (add scores for items 3, 5, 8, 9, 15, and 18)_____
> *Trustworthiness Factor* (add scores for items 4, 6, 11, 12, 14, and 17)_____

Interpretation: Total scores should range between 6 and 42. Scores above 32 indicate high credibility. Scores below 17 indicate low credibility. Scores of 17–32 indicate moderate credibility.

Source: McCroskey, J. C., &Teven, J. J. (1999). Goodwill: A reexamination of the construct and its measurement. *Communication Monographs, 66,* 90–103. Note: Students should be provided only the directions and scales. The remainder of this information is for the teacher only.

Measure of Task Attraction

Directions: The scales below are designed to indicate how you see "Your Teacher" as a person with whom to work. Please indicate the degree to which each statement applies to "Your Teacher" by marking whether you: Strongly Disagree = 1; Disagree = 2; Undecided = 3; Agree = 4; Strongly Agree = 5.

_____ 1. He/she would not be a good person to work with.

_____ 2. You could count on her/him getting the job done.

_____ 3. I have confidence in her/his ability to get the job done.

_____ 4. If I wanted to get things done, I could probably depend on her/him.

_____ 5. I could not get anything accomplished working with her/him.

_____ 6. He/she works hard when assigned a job to do.

Scoring: To compute the score, rescore items 1 and 5 with the following format: $1 = 5; 2 = 4; 3 = 3; 4 = 2; 5 = 1$. Add the scores for the six items. Scores should range from 6 to 30.

Task Attraction Total = _____

Interpretation: Scores above 21 indicate high attractiveness. Scores below 16 indicate low attractiveness. Scores of 16–21 indicate moderate attractiveness.

Source: McCroskey, J. C., & McCain, T. A. (1974). The measurement of interpersonal attraction. *Speech Monographs, 41,* 261–266.

Note: Students should be provided only the directions and scales. The remainder of this information is for the teacher only.

Teacher Clarity Measure

Directions: The scales below are designed to indicate how you think "Your Teacher" communicates information in class. Please indicate the degree to which you agree with each item by marking whether you: Strongly Disagree = 1; Disagree = 2; Undecided = 3; Agree = 4; Strongly Agree = 5.

_____ 1. My teacher clearly defines major concepts.
_____ 2. My teacher's answers to student questions are unclear.
_____ 3. In general, I understand my teacher.
_____ 4. Projects assigned for the class have unclear guidelines.
_____ 5. My teacher's objectives for the course are clear.
_____ 6. My teacher is straightforward in her/his lectures.
_____ 7. My teacher is not clear when defining guidelines for out-of-class assignments.
_____ 8. My teacher uses clear and relevant examples.
_____ 9. In general, I would say that my teacher's classroom communication is unclear.
_____10. My teacher is explicit in her/his instruction.

Scoring:
Step 1. Add the scores for items 1, 3, 5, 6, 8, and 10.
Step 2. Add the scores for items 2, 4, 7, and 9.
Total score: Start with the number 24, then add that to the total from step 1, then subtract the total from step 2.

Interpretation: Scores may range from 10 to 50. Scores above 40 indicate high clarity. Scores below 20 indicate low clarity. Scores of 20–40 indicate moderate clarity.

Source: Chesebro, J. L., and McCroskey, J. C. (1998). The development of the Teacher Clarity Short Inventory (TCSI) to measure clear teaching in the classroom. *Communication Research Reports, 15,* 262–266.

Note: Students should be provided only the directions and the scales. The remainder of this information is for the teacher only.

Teacher Immediacy Measure

Instructions: Below are a series of statements that describe the ways some people behave while talking with or to others. You are asked to indicate how well each statement applies to "Your Teacher's" communication with you. For each statement, choose the number that most closely describes Your Teacher's behavior. Write that number in the space before the number of the statement.

1 = Never; 2 = Rarely; 3 = Occasionally; 4 = Often; 5 = Very Often

_____ 1. Uses hands and arms to gesture while talking to you.

_____ 2. Use a monotone or dull voice while talking to you.

_____ 3. Looks at you while talking to you.

_____ 4. Frowns while talking to you.

_____ 5. Has a very tense body position while talking to you.

_____ 6. Moves away while talking to you.

_____ 7. Uses a variety of vocal expressions while talking to you.

_____ 8. Touches you on the shoulder or arm while talking to you.

_____ 9. Smiles while talking to you.

_____ 10. Looks away from you while talking to you.

_____ 11. Has a relaxed body position while talking to you.

_____ 12. Is "stiff" while talking to you.

_____ 13. Avoids touching you while talking to you.

_____ 14. Moves closer while talking to you.

_____ 15. Is animated while talking to you.

_____ 16. Looks bland or neutral when talking to you.

Scoring:
Step 1. Add the scores for items 2, 4, 5, 6, 10, 12, 13, and 16.
Step 2. Add the scores for items 1, 3, 7, 8, 9, 11, 14, and 15.
Total score: Start with the number 48, add the total from Step 2, then subtract the score from Step 1.

Interpretation: Scores may range from 16 to 90. Scores above 74 indicate high immediacy. Scores below 32 indicate low immediacy. Scores of 32–74 indicate moderate immediacy.

Source: Richmond, V. P., & McCroskey, J. C. (1998). *Nonverbal communication in interpersonal relationships,* 3rd ed. Boston: Allyn & Bacon.

Note: Students should be provided only the directions and the scales. The remainder of this information is for the teacher only.

Assertiveness and Responsiveness Measures

Instructions: The questionnaire below lists 20 characteristics of people. Please indicate the degree to which you believe each of these characteristics applies to "Your Teacher" while interacting with you by marking whether you (5) strongly agree that it applies, (4) agree that it applies, (3) are undecided, (2) disagree that it applies, or (1) strongly disagree that it applies. There are no right or wrong answers. Work quickly; record your first impression.

_____ 1. helpful

_____ 2. defends own beliefs

_____ 3. independent

_____ 4. responsive to others

_____ 5. forceful

_____ 6. has strong personality

_____ 7. sympathetic

_____ 8. compassionate

_____ 9. assertive

_____ 10. sensitive to the needs of others

_____ 11. dominant

_____ 12. sincere

_____ 13. gentle

_____ 14. willing to take a stand

_____ 15. warm

_____ 16. tender

_____ 17. friendly

_____ 18. acts as a leader

_____ 19. aggressive

_____ 20. competitive

Scoring: For the assertiveness score, add responses to items 2, 3, 5, 6, 9, 11, 14, 18, 19, and 20. For the responsiveness score, add responses to items 1, 4, 7, 8, 10, 12, 13, 15, 16, and 17.

Interpretation: Scores may range from 10 to 50 on each measure. Scores above 40 indicate high assertiveness or responsiveness. Scores below 20 indicate low assertiveness or responsiveness. Scores between 20 and 40 indicate moderate assertiveness or responsiveness.

Source: Richmond, V. P., & McCroskey, J. C. (1990). Reliability and separation of factors on the assertiveness-responsiveness scale. *Psychological Reports, 67,* 449–450.

Note: Students should be provided only the directions and scales. The remainder of this information is for the teacher only.

Author Index

Subject Index